Macro Trading and
Investment Strategies

WILEY TRADING ADVANTAGE

Macro Trading and Investment Strategies

Macroeconomic Arbitrage in Global Markets

Gabriel Burstein

John Wiley & Sons, Inc.

New York • Chichester • Weinheim • Brisbane • Singapore • Toronto

Published by John Wiley & Sons, Inc.
Published simultaneously in Canada.

Library of Congress Cataloging-in-Publication Data:

Burstein, Gabriel, 1959–
    Macro trading and investment strategies : macroeconomic arbitrage
in global markets / Gabriel Burstein.
      p. cm. — (Wiley trading advantage)
    ISBN 0-471-31586-9 (cloth : alk. paper)
    1. Arbitrage. 2. Speculation. 3. Hedging (Finance)
4. Macroeconomics 5. Competition, International.   I. Title.
II. Series.
HG6041.B82   1999
332.64'5—dc21   98-39938

Printed in the United States of America.

10 9 8 7 6 5 4 3 2 1

To the brave pioneers of macro hedge fund investment: George Soros, Stanley Druckenmiller, Nick Roditi, Jerry Manolovici, Julian Robertson, Michael Steinhardt, Paul Tudor Jones, Leon Cooperman, Bruce Kovner, Louis Bacon, David Gerstenhaber, Victor Niederhoffer, and to the many other macro soldiers who won or lost on the battle-field of macroeconomic-views-based trading, with my admiration and with the hope that Global Macroeconomic Arbitrage may contribute to opening an objective macroeconomic mispricings arbitrage path as an alternative to subjective macroeconomic-views-based directional trading.

Preface

Global macro investment is undoubtedly perceived as more of an art than a science. Trading and investment styles will never be just science, but one particular style is perceived as being the closest to an art: *global macro*. Although traders have always tried to anticipate the future of currencies and bonds with an eye to macroeconomics, global macro investment started officially when special funds called "macro hedge funds" started to focus systematically on such opportunities as a part of their much broader portfolio of investment strategies. It all started thus with the creators and the managers of the new macro hedge funds: Soros Fund, Tiger, Tudor Jones, Steinhardt, Caxton, Omega, Moore Capital, those referred to in our dedication, and many others we apologize for not mentioning in this brief preface. As a macro proprietary trader at Goldman Sachs, I was of course captivated by all these role models as well as by the macro thinking of prominent strategists like Byron Wien and Barton Biggs at Morgan Stanley or Gavyn Davies at Goldman Sachs who influenced my formation. I understood gradually that there are many more unexploited avenues in macro trading and investment that can bring global macro trading and investment nearer to an investment-strategy science and away from just an investment art, nearer to arbitrage-like strategies and away from pure directional buying. I want to thank Jerry Manolovici for giving me the chance to discuss some of these strategies with him after the completion of the manuscript. Gary Crowder of Tiger made me realize clearly that global macro as a strategy is only one of the many things a macro hedge fund follows.

Preface

As head of a long/short relative value and macro European equity sales group that I set up at Daiwa Europe to cover hedge fund clients with new strategies and execution and as a frequent speaker on new macro strategies at hedge fund conferences, I realized that fewer and fewer new macro hedge funds open and that the average hedge fund investor, private or institutional, has a very limited understanding of the functionality and possibilities of macro hedge fund investment strategies, which contributes to a deformed and unfair representation. By formalizing for the first time in a book the directional and long/short strategies used in macro trading and investment, I hope to have contributed to the filling of this knowledge gap, leading thus to more accurate and fair representations of the global macro style and to a higher investment appetite in macro hedge funds. I hope that hedge fund managers, proprietary traders, strategists, economists, and institutional and private investors will try to explore global macroeconomics arbitrage, the new original type of strategy introduced in this book, as a possible way to discover new macro strategies and to reduce the risk in macro trading and investment.

This book is a rare opportunity to look back on my career and my life and to express my gratitude to all those who helped and educated me. I start of course with my mother and father, Edith and Israel, who taught me that one of the main goals of existence is creative research and discovery. Like George Soros, I came from Eastern Europe, in more recent but still difficult times. His story of success and determination proved to me how a handicap can turn into an advantage. I want to thank again Eva Mitchell, Ferdy Beck, the whole of WJR, and Professor M. Davis for their help and support. Gavyn Davies, Chief Economist at Goldman Sachs, and Mike O'Brien gave me the chance to start my education about markets actively as a proprietary trader at Goldman Sachs. Omar Dobouny, Danny Och, Sushil Wadhwany, Abbey Cohen, and David Morrison were great teachers, and I am very grateful to them. I want to thank Gavyn Davies for his constant support in those beginning days. My activity at Daiwa Europe owes a lot to the entrepreneurial spirit of Michael Watson and Itsuki Shibusawa as well as to working together in a team with brilliant professionals like Bernard Godement, Mike Buhl-Nielsen, Don Eggington, Naz Craft, Steve Turi,

Preface

Philip Jordan, Jerry Walsh, Tony Gibbons, and of course, Mark Edwards. Lois Peltz at Managed Account Reports (MAR), Aaron Gay and Jonathan McIlroy at Alternative Investment Conferences (AIC), Laura Garza at International Institute for Research (IIR), and Abe Wellington at Opal repeatedly offered me the invaluable chance to present and to discuss my macroeconomic arbitrage strategies at the hedge fund conferences they organized so well. I am grateful to Joseph Nicholas, Michael Kimbarovski, and Cindi Galiano at Hedge Fund Research, who gave me the permission to use one of their famous pie charts; to Datastream and Steve Hartman, who gave me permission to use their database and graphic software to build my strategies; and to Lars Hamich at Deutsche Borse, who gave me permission to use the STOXX index data. Thanks to my sister and my brother-in-law, Monica and Sorin Moise, for their volunteer expert computer support, and to Sharon Grosser, for positive thinking sessions during the writing of this book. Last but not least, this book is the result of my John Wiley editor, Pamela van Giessen, and her assistants, Claudio Campuzano and Mary Todd, welcoming me with hospitality and insight into their Trading Advantage Series. I want to thank Pamela, associate managing editor Mary Daniello, copy editor Judy Cardanha, and Maggie Dana at Pageworks, for all their work and particularly for their patience.

Finally, a special word about the unusual global markets turmoil that developed and worsened as I was writing this book. When I finished the manuscript and handed it to John Wiley & Sons, hardly did I know that the Asian crisis would be so quickly followed by the collapse of Russia, the shaking of Latin America, and the hedge funds crisis. All I knew from the "1994 markets" experience was that in periods when markets are difficult, it is hard to trade on macroeconomic views only. Liquidity disappears and everybody gets hurt because of trading identical, similar, or just correlated strategies. New noncorrelated investment strategies based on objective mispricings rather than subjective views are particularly needed in such difficult markets. This book is devoted to developing one such new strategy: *global macroeconomic arbitrage*.

GABRIEL BURSTEIN
London, England

Contents

Contents

Chapter 1

Introduction: From Subjective Macroeconomic Views to Objective Macroeconomic Mispricings in Global Markets

Macroeconomic Views and Mispricings

T his book is about macroeconomics-based trading and investment strategies in global markets. We will present the classical global macro strategies and introduce our new original macroeconomic arbitrage strategies to which the main core of the book is dedicated. Traditionally, macroeconomic views on economic variables and indicators (interest rates, consumer price index [CPI], gross domestic product [GDP]) are used to formulate market views on the corresponding assets (bonds, currencies, stock indices), driven by those variables and indicators. We will formulate, analyze, and give examples of the strategies known as *global macro strategies*, covering both the directional macro strategies (based on directional views on individual assets leading to either buying/overweighting or selling/underweighting decisions) and long/short macro strategies (based on relative views on two related and similar assets or group of assets leading to simultaneously buying/overweighting the one expected to outperform and selling short/ underweighting the one expected to underperform). Long/short macro strategies focus thus on spreads between related assets, betting on the relation between two related similar assets rather than on the direction of a single asset, as directional macro strategies do.

The main focus and original contribution of this book is the intro- duction of a new type of macro trading and investment strategies that are based on macroeconomics mispricings in global markets: *global macroeconomic arbitrage*. This is a new type of global long/short macro strategy that is based on detecting objective macroeconomic mispricings: mispriced representations of macroeconomic variables, indicators, and relations among these in the corresponding relations among assets in global markets. The difference between traditional global macro and our original macroeconomic arbitrage is the difference between subjective macroeconomic views and objective macroeconomic mispricings. A macroeconomic mispricing (see Figure 1.1) is a hole or a gap between markets and underlying explanatory macroeconomics. Figure 1.1 represents symbolically the relation between market prices of assets (bonds, currencies, stock indices) and the value of driving

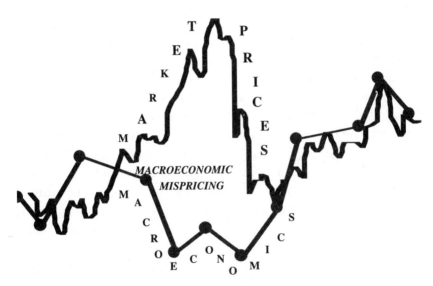

Figure 1.1

Symbolic representation of a macroeconomic mispricing in markets (explanation of cover design). Market prices of assets (bonds, equities, currencies) are influenced by some essential macroeconomic variables and indicators. Correct pricing and tracking of macroeconomics by market prices of assets is sometimes interrupted by "mispricing gaps," when the two diverge from each other only to reconverge later in time. This gap or hole is what will be referred to in this book as a *macroeconomic mispricing*. This is the image that in different markets and specific situations will be seen everywhere in the book.

underlying explanatory macroeconomic variables or indicators. Correct pricing of macroeconomics in the market is represented by periods when market prices track the value of the underlying macroeconomic variables. Mispricings are represented by clear gaps where market prices diverge from the underlying macroeconomics. In fact, Figure 1.1's interpretation can be generalized to encompass relations among assets such as in particular spreads versus relations (for example, ratios) among underlying macroeconomic variables and indicators. It is this generalization that led us to the new type of macroeconomic arbitrage strategies in which macro relations mispricings in market asset relations are being objectively detected and arbitraged.

This book was written as visually as possible: rather than illustrating the text we spread the text around and inside illustrations. I tried as much as possible to explain and to put my thoughts and methods in a graphic or symbolic form.

One will find in our examples a dominant echo of the impact on global markets of the recent Asian crisis, as well as the past, present, and future influence of the introduction of a single European currency in the final phase of the creation in 1999 of the European Monetary Union (EMU), with its immediate implication: the creation of a unified EMU-Eurozone market. The macro style of trading and investment was dominated by these events, and it seemed obvious to apply our new macroeconomic arbitrage theory and strategies to these major events in global markets while covering opportunities created by macroeconomic mispricings in the United States, the United Kingdom, France, Germany, Spain, and Italy.

Our approach while focusing on macroeconomic fundamentals tried to be simultaneously technical and quantitative. Economic indicators, trendlines and double tops, rolling correlations, regressions, and volatilities all play their roles in the new macroeconomic arbitrage method, which detects opportunities that are not so transparent to everybody because of the lack of a joint unified approach by these tools.

Chapter 2

Macro Trading and Investment Strategies

Trading and investment based primarily (but not exclusively!) on macroeconomic information and macroeconomic views are known as *macro trading and investment.* The distinction we make here between trading and investment is based on the difference between short- and medium-term trading and long-term investing. Strategies with such predominant macroeconomic motivation are called *macro strategies.* These are top-down bets on macroeconomic themes using liquid assets in large volumes. Hedge funds following this approach are called *macro hedge funds,* and they are characterized by a macro style of trading and investment overlayed on other globally diversified strategies. It is important to understand that the portfolio of strategies of a global macro hedge fund is much wider than just global macro strategies. This book deals with intrinsic global macro strategies and not with global macro hedge fund styles as a whole. In the universe of assets of hedge funds, macro style has the largest asset allocation among all other strategies or styles, such as market neutral, relative value arbitrage, merger arbitrage, and distressed securities, as shown in Figure 2.1.

The typical instruments used to implement such strategies are currencies, bond and stock index futures, commodities, and interest rate futures. Traditionally, the main macroeconomic themes focused on interest rates, inflation consumer price index (CPI), producer price index (PPI), gross domestic product (GDP), exchange rates, and money supply. Simplifying matters just for the moment, a typical example of macro trades is that whatever macroeconomic indicator or variable one watches (CPI, PPI, retail sales, GDP, employment), one generally ends up drawing a conclusion on the trend of interest rates based on growth and inflation. From here one infers either bullish or bearish directional conclusions on currencies (exchange rate), stock indices, and bonds. It is important to note from this early stage that a macroeconomic indicator like retail sales was used thus far as an intermediary tool to assess inflation and almost never as a direct theme for a macro trade. One of the main contributions of this book will be *to refocus the macro style on all the auxiliary macro indicators and variables and to generate new strategies using assets directly related to these* (example: retailers stocks trades based on retail sales mispricing in stock markets as opposed to stock index futures trades based on inflation expectations using retail sales as a variable in the thinking process leading to views on inflation).

Macro trading and investment strategies started and developed historically as directional strategies, when one typically buys an asset because several macroeconomic variables and indicators lead to macroeconomic views favorable to that asset. This is why macro has high volatility and high returns (see Figure 2.2). It was probably in fixed-income markets that macroeconomic information was first used to lead to nondirectional long/short macro trades and investments when, simultaneously with buying an asset, a second related similar asset was also sold against the first one, based on relative performance expectations given by macroeconomic views. Examples of this would be selling a government bond of one country against a government bond of a related country based on relative interest-rate expectations and selling long term bonds against bonds with shorter maturities (known as *yield curve trades*) based, for example, on the pattern of growth. Long/short macro trades have lower returns than directional trades do, but also lower volatility. The difference between long/short macro trading and long/short macro investment is that the latter can also be implemented as an overweight/underweight investment rebalancing in addition to the usual buying/short selling. We said that macro started historically as a top-down approach. However, a lot of the macro players are stock pickers using not just the valuation of the company but, for example, its exposure to some macro variable, such as exchange rates or interest rates (example: buying dollar-sensitive stocks or

Figure 2.1

Hedge fund assets allocation on different strategies (styles). Macro is the dominating slice of the pie with 20.5 percent. The term *arbitrage* was until now associated with merger arbitrage, convertible arbitrage, and relative value arbitrage. It is the objective of this book to intro-duce *macroeconomic arbitrage* as a new type of arbitrage associated with the macro strategy (style).

Hedge Fund Assets Allocation on Strategies through December 1997

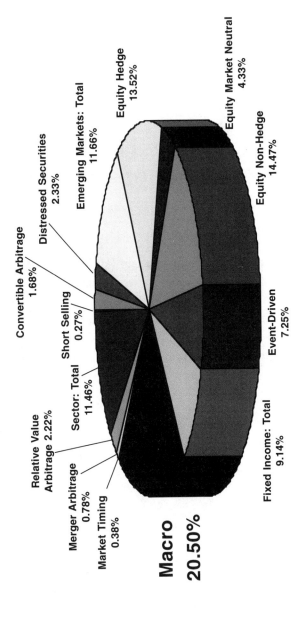

Convertible Arbitrage 1.68%

Distressed Securities 2.33%

Emerging Markets: Total 11.66%

Equity Hedge 13.52%

Equity Market Neutral 4.33%

Equity Non-Hedge 14.47%

Short Selling 0.27%

Sector: Total 11.46%

Relative Value Arbitrage 2.22%

Merger Arbitrage 0.78%

Market Timing 0.38%

Macro 20.50%

Fixed Income: Total 9.14%

Event-Driven 7.25%

Source: Hedge Fund Research, Inc., 312-685-0955, www.hfr.com. Copyright 1997. All rights reserved.

Figure 2.2

Macro trading and investment strategy (style) definition and types:
Top-down bets on macroeconomic themes (based on macroeconomic
views), which are generally opportunistic and directional and involve
large volumes in liquid assets. Macro strategies can also be long/short
in order to have a lower volatility than the directional macro or just
because they are based on an outperformance bet on one asset versus
another. Macro strategies are characterized by high returns and high
volatilities.

TOP-DOWN BETS ON MACROECONOMIC THEMES

HIGH RETURNS

HIGH VOLATILITY

MACRO

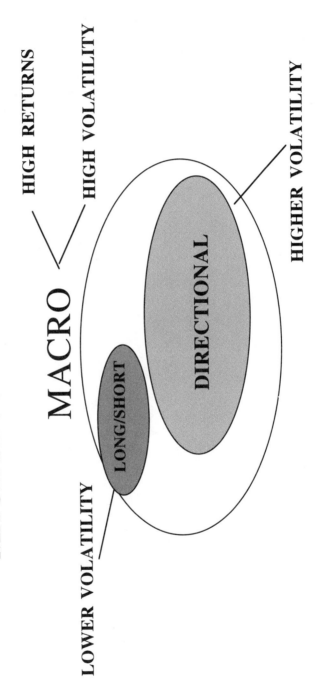

HIGHER VOLATILITY

LOWER VOLATILITY

LONG/SHORT

DIRECTIONAL

interest-rate-sensitive stocks). In stock markets, macro was implemented with stock index futures or with macro stock-picking techniques at the stock level (micro level). In between macro and micro, in between the market level and the stock level, macro very often forgot to exploit the intermediate sector level and particularly macroeconomic relations between sectors. This book will fill this gap with new original strategies based on detecting macroeconomic mispricings.

Chapter **3**

Directional Macro Trading
and Investment

D irectional macro trading and investment involves either buying or selling short an asset based on views and expectations on underlying macroeconomic variables that influence the dynamics of that asset price. We formalize in Figure 3.1 the theoretical model of *directional macro trading*: the strategy by which bullish macroeconomic views and expectations lead to buying representative assets thus establishing long positions and by which bearish macroeconomic views and expectations lead to short selling strategies of representative assets thus establishing short positions. In *directional macro investment* there also exists the possibility to overweight (increase) long- and medium-term positions in assets favored by our macroeconomic views and similarly to underweight (decrease) positions in assets expected to be affected negatively given our macroeconomic expectations and views.

In Europe in 1999, the final stage of the European Monetary Union (EMU) will be implemented: the single currency will be introduced. This was the reason for one of the most successful and popular macro directional trades. Introduction of a single European currency was only possible if the interest rates of the 11 countries that join the EMU would have converged to German rates, the anchor of the EMU, by 1999 (Euroconvergence). Italy and Spain were the high yielders of Europe, and rates in these two countries had the farthest to fall in order for the Euroconvergence to be achieved (see Figure 3.2). Falling short-term rates lead to rallies in stock markets, so Italy and Spain were the best equity markets to be in ahead of the final phase of the EMU commencing in 1999. We can see in Figure 3.3 how the Italian stock market index almost doubled from June 1997 to March 1998 and how it outperformed all major European stock indices. The best recent European directional macro trade and investment strategy was to be long (to buy) Italian financial and interest-rate-sensitive stocks or simply to buy Italian stock index futures (MIB 30). Figure 3.4 shows how views and expectations on short-term rates in Italy led to bullish (buy/overweight) macro views and expectations on the Italian stock index as the representative asset that will benefit the most from the fall in rates. It is of course not as simple as it looks now: it was not a smooth ride because Italian political crises and the risk that Italy will not satisfy the debt/gross domestic product ratio condition of the EMU kept appearing, disappearing, and then reappearing again.

Figure 3.1

Directional macro trading and investment based on macroeconomic views. A long (bullish/buy) or short (bearish/sell) directional position is taken in an asset (bond, currency, stock index) based on views on a certain underlying macroeconomic variable or indicator (interest rates, inflation, etc.). Macro investment is based on medium- to long-term views, whereas macro trading involves short- to medium-term views.

(Original figure designed and analyzed by the author using Datastream database and graphics.)

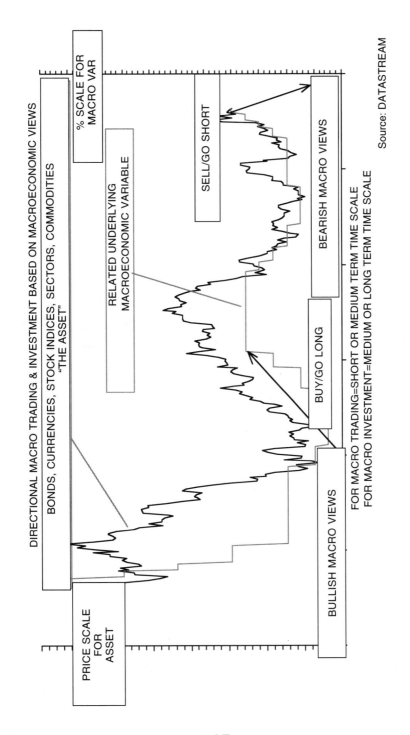

DIRECTIONAL MACRO TRADING & INVESTMENT BASED ON MACROECONOMIC VIEWS

BONDS, CURRENCIES, STOCK INDICES, SECTORS, COMMODITIES
"THE ASSET"

% SCALE FOR
MACRO VAR

RELATED UNDERLYING
MACROECONOMIC VARIABLE

SELL/GO SHORT

BEARISH MACRO VIEWS

BUY/GO LONG

BULLISH MACRO VIEWS

PRICE SCALE
FOR
ASSET

FOR MACRO TRADING=SHORT OR MEDIUM TERM TIME SCALE
FOR MACRO INVESTMENT=MEDIUM OR LONG TERM TIME SCALE

Source: DATASTREAM

Figure 3.2

Euroconvergence ahead of the 1999 beginning of the single currency phase of the European Monetary Union (EMU). Italy and Spain were the high yielders that had to fall the farthest to converge to the already realigned French and German rates ahead of the 1999 final stage of EMU, when the single European currency will be introduced. Italian rates had to fall farther than the Spanish ones.

(Original figure designed and analyzed by the author using Datastream database and graphics.)

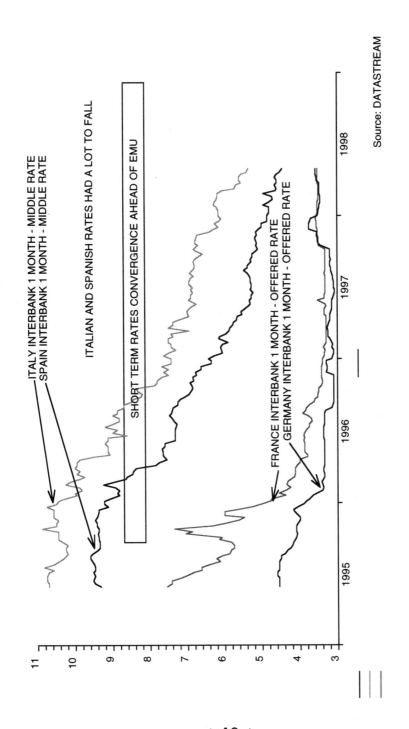

ITALY INTERBANK 1 MONTH - MIDDLE RATE
SPAIN INTERBANK 1 MONTH - MIDDLE RATE

ITALIAN AND SPANISH RATES HAD A LOT TO FALL

SHORT TERM RATES CONVERGENCE AHEAD OF EMU

FRANCE INTERBANK 1 MONTH - OFFERED RATE
GERMANY INTERBANK 1 MONTH - OFFERED RATE

Source: DATASTREAM

Figure 3.3

The Euroconvergence-driven fall in interest rates led to rallies in the stock indices of Italy and Spain. By March 1998, Italian stock indices (COMIT 30, MIB 30) almost doubled compared to the previous year and outperformed Spain's IBEX and the other core EMU stock indices, like France's CAC 40 and Germany's DAX. This was due to the fall and *expectation of further fall* in interest rates.

(Original figure designed and analyzed by the author using Datastream database and graphics.)

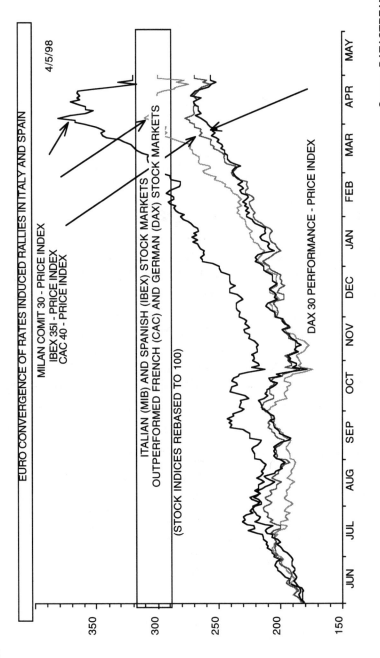

EURO CONVERGENCE OF RATES INDUCED RALLIES IN ITALY AND SPAIN

MILAN COMIT 30 - PRICE INDEX
IBEX 35I - PRICE INDEX
CAC 40 - PRICE INDEX

4/5/98

ITALIAN (MIB) AND SPANISH (IBEX) STOCK MARKETS
OUTPERFORMED FRENCH (CAC) AND GERMAN (DAX) STOCK MARKETS

(STOCK INDICES REBASED TO 100)

DAX 30 PERFORMANCE - PRICE INDEX

JUN JUL AUG SEP OCT NOV DEC JAN FEB MAR APR MAY

350   300   250   200   150

Source: DATASTREAM

♦ 21 ♦

Figure 3.4

Macro directional trade/investment based on Euroconvergence views on interest rates ahead of the 1999 single-currency, final phase of the European monetary union (EMU): Buy Italian equities (futures on stock index MIB 30 or financial interest-rate-sensitive stocks). The Euroconvergence views on short rates in Italy (Italian rates had to fall to converge to the German and the French core EMU rates) led to bullish views on the Italian stock market in general and on financial interest-rate-sensitive stocks in particular. A fall in short-term interest rates leads to a rally in the stock market (inverse proportional relation), as shown in the chart where the Italian COMIT 30 stock index tracks (100 − Italian discount rate) (inverse of short rate): only 4 percent rate cuts and particularly expectation of more to come led to 100 percent profits in a long directional macro position in the Italian stock index.

(Original figure designed and analyzed by the author using Datastream database and graphics.)

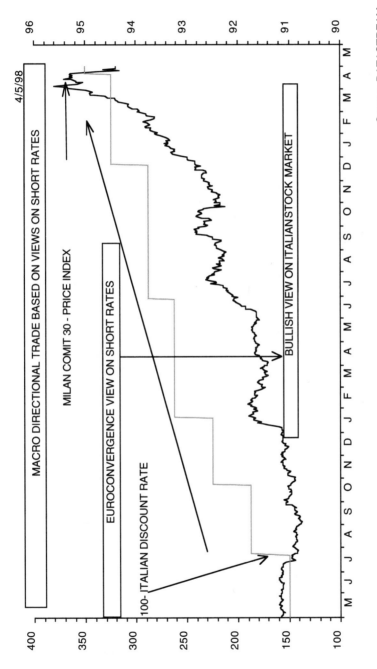

MACRO DIRECTIONAL TRADE BASED ON VIEWS ON SHORT RATES

MILAN COMIT 30 - PRICE INDEX

EUROCONVERGENCE VIEW ON SHORT RATES

100 - ITALIAN DISCOUNT RATE

BULLISH VIEW ON ITALIAN STOCK MARKET

4/5/98

Source: DATASTREAM

Chapter 4

Long/Short Macro Trading and Investment

Long/short macro trading and investment is a type of macro strategy that involves buying one asset and simultaneously selling short another asset (also referred to as taking a position in the spread between the two assets), thus betting on the direction of this spread using macroeconomic views indicating that the former asset should outperform the latter. Although this strategy can be successful in trending bull markets, we would like to present it as probably the crucial macro strategy in nontrending markets, when uncertainty is bigger than ever. As we saw in Chapter 3, directional macro involves betting on the direction (trend) of an asset using macroeconomic information. If the markets are nontrending due to, for example, the surprise and uncertainty created by the U.S. Federal Reserve (the Fed) raising rates in 1994 (Figure 4.1) or due to the unpredictability of the unfolding of the Asian crisis in 1997 and 1998 (Figure 4.2), it becomes very difficult to implement directional strategies because, even if the macroeconomic trend is correctly assessed, the lack of immediate technical trend (market direction), the lack of any pattern, and the broken normal relations between assets (see Figures 4.2 and 4.3) lead to large swings, making it impossible to carry, for example, a long position consistently throughout a macro trade in "difficult markets." Macro directional trading is hard to implement in a *difficult* market, which is characterized by lack of trend and pattern as well as by counterintuitive relations between assets. In 1994, the Standard & Poor's (S&P) 500 had no trend (direction) and no pattern after an upward trending 1993 when the market rallied in an upward channel pattern (see Figure 4.1). The same situation appeared in 1997: after an incredible bull market period with clear direction, the Asian crisis eliminated any trend and pattern from U.S. markets. The only trending markets were the Asian downtrending markets. Macro trades involving selling short Asia were very successful, whereas directional macro trading in the United States and Europe was much more difficult. What made any macro trading and investment even more difficult in 1997 and 1998 was the collapse of the normal positive correlation between bonds and equities (Figure 4.3). Even if during some short periods bonds outperform equities and over long-term horizons equities outperform bonds, the two classes of assets remain positively correlated.

During the fall of the Asian markets, any weak noninflationary macroeconomic data (low industrial production, for example), which used to be positive for both stocks and bonds, was interpreted as negative for equities, given the slowing growth and thus the decreasing earnings perspective. At the same time, bonds were rallying due to the noninflationary interpretation but also due to the switch out of equities into bonds. This caused the collapse of the positive correlation between bonds and equities: bonds and equities became negatively correlated assets like commodities and equities. The negative correlation, the switch out of equities into bonds, made bonds and equities compete for demand flows in markets. In this way trends evaporated because market-stable direction, among others, develops through a reciprocal long-lived enhancement mechanism between assets rather than through short-lived competition between assets, which breaks any emerging trends.

Long/short macro strategies are one possible solution for difficult markets. The idea is to replace a directional view/expectation on an asset correlated with the direction of market by a macroeconomic-information-based bet on a two-asset spread that is noncorrelated with the market. It is as if we refocused from the direction of the market to the direction of a new synthetic asset (the spread) whose direction has no correlation with the direction of market. The model of long/short macro investment and trading strategy is shown in Figure 4.4: views on a spread (ratio) between two assets or between two groups of assets

Figure 4.1

Directional macro is hard to implement in a "difficult market"—a market without trend and with no pattern. S&P 500 in 1994 became a "difficult market" (without trend and with no pattern), after the Fed raised rates unexpectedly. Directional macro strategies, which were so successful in the previous year in a trending market with an upward channel pattern, did not survive the unforgettable 1994, almost as unforgettable as 1987 and the 1997–1998 Asian crisis.

(Original figure designed and analyzed by the author using Datastream database and graphics.)

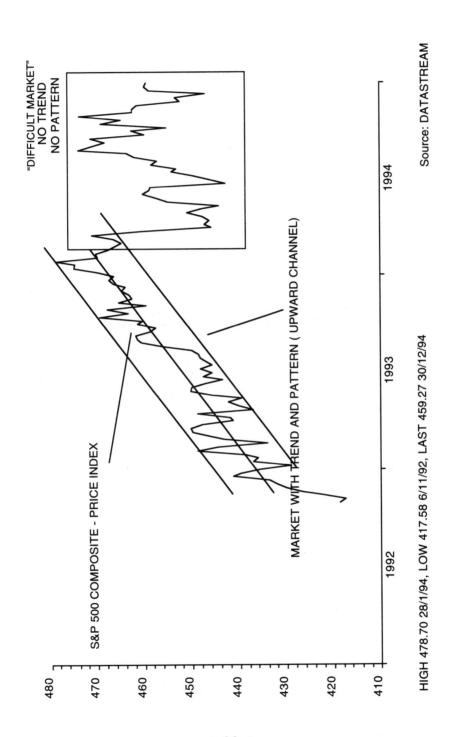

"DIFFICULT MARKET"
NO TREND
NO PATTERN

S&P 500 COMPOSITE - PRICE INDEX

MARKET WITH TREND AND PATTERN (UPWARD CHANNEL)

480
470
460
450
440
430
420
410

1992   1993   1994

HIGH 478.70 28/1/94, LOW 417.58 6/11/92, LAST 459.27 30/12/94

Source: DATASTREAM

Figure 4.2

June 1996–July 1997, a great period for directional macro strategies, was followed by the difficult market conditions of the Asian crisis: no trend, no pattern, and broken normal relations between assets. The only markets having trend during the Asian crisis were the Asian markets themselves trending down. Directional long or short macro strategies had a difficult time in the United States and Europe, whereas macro short strategies in Asia performed well, taking advantage of the clear downtrend.

(Original figure designed and analyzed by the author using Datastream database and graphics.)

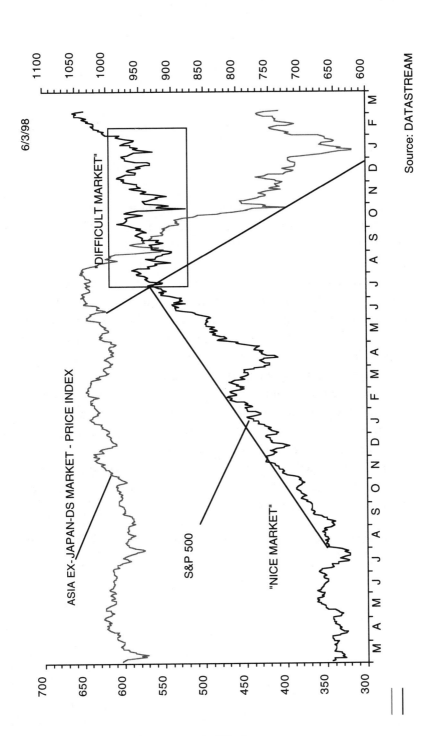

6/3/98

DIFFICULT MARKET"

ASIA EX- JAPAN-DS MARKET - PRICE INDEX

S&P 500

"NICE MARKET"

Source: DATASTREAM

Figure 4.3

Besides the existence of trend and pattern, the existence of normal relations between assets is another condition that enables successful implementation of macro directional strategies. The normal positive correlation between bonds and equities was broken during the Asian crisis. Even if bonds are outperforming or equities are outperforming, they remain historically positively correlated with each other under normal market conditions. The figure shows how the rolling positive correlation between benchmark bond futures and stock index futures in the United States, France, Germany, and the United Kingdom collapsed and became negative during the 1997–1998 Asian crisis. The explanation originates in the United States where noninflationary macroeconomic data, always good for bonds and stocks, were now interpreted to signal slowing growth and, thus, contracting corporate earnings due to Asia. Stocks were hurt due to earnings fears, whereas bonds outperformed in an avalanche of noninflationary macroeconomic data. The negative correlation was enhanced by investors switching out of equities into bonds.

(Original figure designed and analyzed by the author using Datastream database and graphics.)

DIFFICULT MARKET=NORMAL RELATIONS BETWEEN ASSETS ARE BROKEN

3MTH MOVING CORRELATIONS BETWEEN BOND FUTURE AND STOCK INDEX FUTURE
IN US,FRANCE,GERMANY,UK

THE COLLAPSE OF BOND-EQUITY CORRELATION

Source: DATASTREAM

(two stock indices, two sectors, etc.) are formed based on macroeconomic views on a related underlying macro variable or indicator. Bullish macro views suggest bullish views on the spread A-B (or ratio A/B) leading to buying the spread, that is, to buying A and selling B. Bearish macro views produce bearish views on the spread A-B leading to selling A and buying B. Long/short macro investment strategies can be implemented by portfolio managers as an overweight/underweight strategy in which one overweighs the asset expected to outperform and underweighs the other asset.

In Figure 4.5, we consider a long/short macro trading strategy (or overweight/underweight macro investment strategy) based on the analysis of Figure 3.3 and Figure 3.4 on interest rate convergence ahead of the 1999 single-currency final stage of the European Monetary Union (EMU): long Italy (MIB 30 stock index futures)/short Germany (DAX stock index futures). This is a strategy exploiting the convergence of Italian rates to the German rates (the "anchor" of EMU), which implied big rate cuts in Italy and very little or none in Germany. Therefore, in a falling-interest-rate environment, the Italian stock market was expected to perform much better than the German one. We can see in Figure 4.5 how Italian equities outperformed German equities by 20 percent from June 1997 to June 1998, while the differential between Italian short rates (one-month interbank rate) and German short rates narrowed by 1.75 percent (or 175 basis points). It was not a smooth, easy trade: we saw Italian political crises and difficulties in approving the new long-term budget ensuring Italy's entry into the EMU in the first wave of 11 countries. That is where trading techniques allowed trading in and out of the Italy/Germany (MIB 30/DAX) spread while keeping a stop loss below the upward support trend of this spread.

We end this chapter by considering another long/short macro strategy that shows the importance of additional macro variables in structuring macro trades. We have so far considered a spread of two assets and an underlying driving macroeconomic variable influencing the balance between the two assets. What if there are two macroeconomic variables influencing the balance between the two assets? Consider again the Euroconvergence process during which the interest rates of

Italy and Spain will converge to German rates, the anchor or the best candidate for the central rate of the EMU, which will see in 1999 the beginning of the European single monetary policy and the introduction of a single European currency. Ahead of 1999, Italian and Spanish rates have fallen, but the differential between them (shown in Figure 4.6 at 100 basis points [bps] or 1 percent in June 1998) has been preserved, although this too has to go due to interest-rate convergence. The ratio between the Italian stock index, COMIT 30, and the Spanish stock index, IBEX, has built in a bullish head-and-shoulders base pattern waiting to erupt in an outperformance rally of Italy over Spain (Figure 4.6). We believe that the bigger rate cuts expected in Italy compared to Spain will be the catalyst of such an Italian outperformance rally. This belief is firmed up by analyzing in Figure 4.6 the gross domestic product (GDP) growth difference between Italy and Spain, the other macroeconomic variable playing an essential role in shaping the evolution of the stock index price ratio between Italy and Spain. The lack until recently of Italian outperformance over Spain can be explained by the faster Spanish growth counterbalancing the larger rate fall expected in Italy. However, Italian GDP growth has caught up with Spanish GDP growth recently. This analysis shows the importance of considering multiple macroeconomic variables in the design of long/short macro investment and trading strategies, a point that will be further elaborated in Chapter 8. Figure 4.6 is also a perfect example of the advantages of combining macroeconomic fundamental analysis with technical analysis, which is one of the main features of our approach throughout this book. In this particular case, technical analysis gives us the entry point into the long Italy/short Spain macro trade—after the break of the bullish head-and-shoulders base in the Italian stock index/Spanish stock index ratio (spread) shown in Figure 4.6. This can happen, for example, when Spain says that there is no more room for rate cuts and Italy cuts rates. Political crises in Italy or reassessment of its GDP can trigger up-and-down moves in the spread before the neckline of the head-and-shoulders base is broken, so there is no reason to be in this trade before this bullish base formation is broken.

Figure 4.4

Long/short macro trading and investment based on macroeconomic views. As opposed to directional macro, in which a position is taken in one asset (Figure 3.1), in long/short macro trading a position is taken in a spread between two related assets (stock indices, sectors, bonds) corresponding to views on an underlying common macroeconomic variable or on a spread/ratio of related macroeconomic variables. Taking a position on (buying) a spread between two assets amounts to buying one asset and selling short the other one, thus creating a long/short position. If the macro views are bullish, the spread is bought; if the macro views are bearish, the spread is sold.

(Original figure designed and analyzed by the author using Datastream database and graphics.)

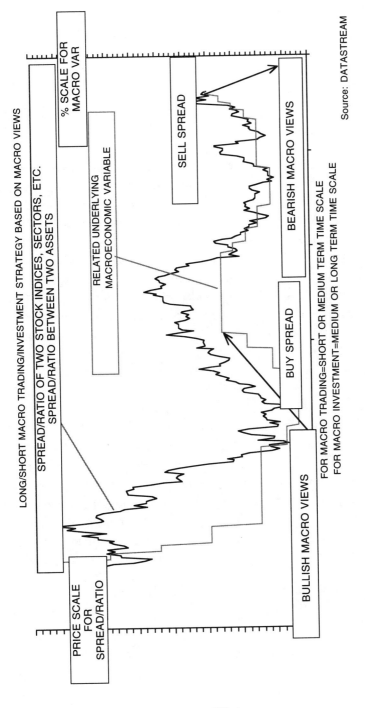

LONG/SHORT MACRO TRADING/INVESTMENT STRATEGY BASED ON MACRO VIEWS

SPREAD/RATIO OF TWO STOCK INDICES, SECTORS, ETC.
SPREAD/RATIO BETWEEN TWO ASSETS

% SCALE FOR MACRO VAR

RELATED UNDERLYING MACROECONOMIC VARIABLE

SELL SPREAD

BEARISH MACRO VIEWS

BUY SPREAD

BULLISH MACRO VIEWS

FOR MACRO TRADING=SHORT OR MEDIUM TERM TIME SCALE
FOR MACRO INVESTMENT=MEDIUM OR LONG TERM TIME SCALE

PRICE SCALE FOR SPREAD/RATIO

Source: DATASTREAM

♦ 37 ♦

Figure 4.5

Long/short (overweight/underweight) macro trading (investment) strategy based on Euroconvergence ahead of the EMU: long (overweight) Italian stockmarket/short (underweight) German stockmarket. Ahead of the 1999 entry of Italy in the first wave of the EMU, we saw (Figure 3.2) that Italian rates were expected to fall and converge to German rates. A falling-interest-rates environment is positive for equities and definitely positive for an overweighted-in-financials (interest-rate-sensitive) market like Italy. In Figure 3.4 it was shown how this leads to a macro directional trade: long (overweight) Italian stocks. An alternative conclusion to be inferred from Figure 3.2 is that Italy should outperform Germany as the spread between Italian and German rates was expected to narrow. This leads us to a long/short (overweight/underweight) macro trading (investment) strategy: long (overweight) Italian stockmarket (MIB 30 futures or financials)/short (underweight) German stockmarket (DAX futures or financials). We can see that the spread MIB 30/DAX rallied by 20 percent over one year suggesting it was a good macro investment strategy for a one-year time horizon. As a long/short macro trading strategy we can see that a support upward trendline was created that could have been used to give a stop-profit-taking signal if the support were significantly broken. We can see that, indeed, Italy outperformed Germany while the spread between German rates and Italian rates narrowed.

(Original strategy and figure designed and analyzed by the author using Datastream database and graphics.)

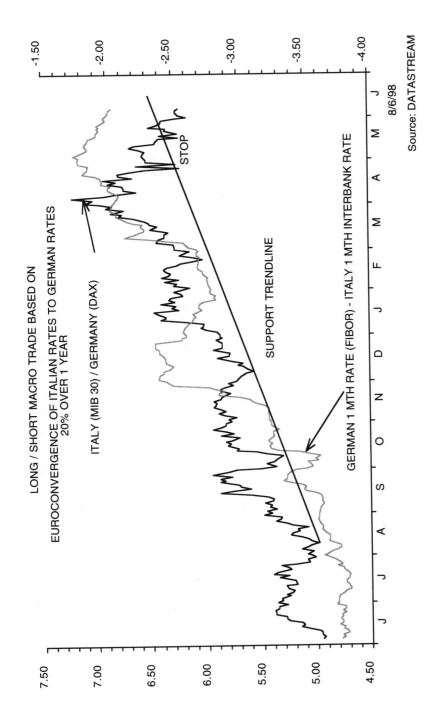

LONG / SHORT MACRO TRADE BASED ON

EUROCONVERGENCE OF ITALIAN RATES TO GERMAN RATES
20% OVER 1 YEAR

ITALY (MIB 30) / GERMANY (DAX)

STOP

SUPPORT TRENDLINE

GERMAN 1 MTH RATE (FIBOR) - ITALY 1 MTH INTERBANK RATE

8/6/98

Source: DATASTREAM

♦ 39 ♦

Figure 4.6

Long/short macro strategy based on the convergence of Italian rates to Spanish rates during the Euroconvergence to EMU "anchor" German rates: buy Italian interest-rate-sensitive financials or stock index futures (MIB)/sell Spanish interest-rate-sensitive financials or stock index futures (IBEX). Italian rates had farther to fall than Spanish rates did in order to converge to German rates (the anchor, or central, rate for the EMU) ahead of the 1999 beginning of the final phase of the EMU. However, although both Italian and Spanish rates have fallen ahead of the 1999 EMU, the difference or gap between them did not narrow. Italian rates will have to fall by 100 bps more than Spanish rates. This indicates that Italian equities should outperform Spanish equities, and, indeed, a very bullish head-and-shoulders base has been formed in the ratio Italian COMIT 30 stock index/Spanish IBEX stock index, which should break and lead to an outperformance rally of Italy over Spain as the Italian rates start falling by 100 bps (1 percent) more than the Spanish ones. There is an additional macro variable, GDP growth, that has to be taken into account. Spain grew much faster than Italy, which explains why Italian corporate earnings did not look as attractive as the Spanish ones and why as a consequence Italy did not outperform Spain until recently. While GDP growth is correctly priced in the Italy/Spain stock index ratio, the 100 bps more rate cuts in Italy should turn the balance in favor of Italy and break the head-and-shoulders bullish base.

(Original strategy and figure designed and analyzed by the author using Datastream database and graphics.)

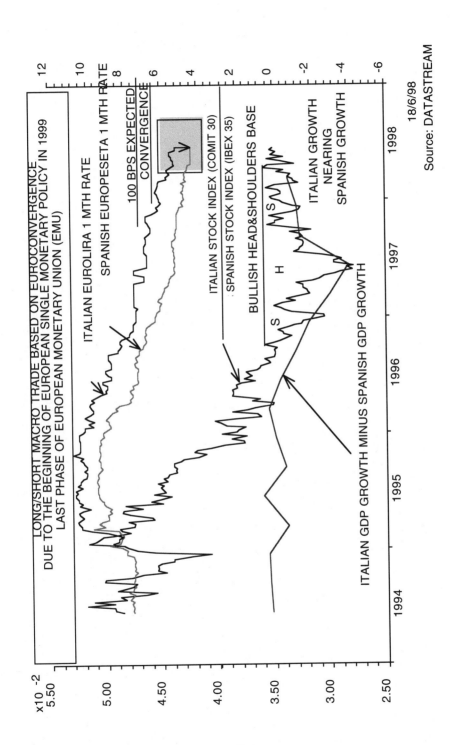

LONG/SHORT MACRO TRADE BASED ON EUROCONVERGENCE
DUE TO THE BEGINNING OF EUROPEAN SINGLE MONETARY POLICY IN 1999
LAST PHASE OF EUROPEAN MONETARY UNION (EMU)

ITALIAN EUROLIRA 1 MTH RATE
SPANISH EUROPESETA 1 MTH RATE

100 BPS EXPECTED
CONVERGENCE

ITALIAN STOCK INDEX (COMIT 30)
SPANISH STOCK INDEX (IBEX 35)

BULLISH HEAD&SHOULDERS BASE

S   H

S

ITALIAN GROWTH
NEARING
SPANISH GROWTH

ITALIAN GDP GROWTH MINUS SPANISH GDP GROWTH

x10 -2
5.50
5.00
4.50
4.00
3.50
3.00
2.50

12
10
8
6
4
2
0
-2
-4
-6

1994   1995   1996   1997   1998

18/6/98

Source: DATASTREAM

Chapter **5**

Macroeconomic Arbitrage in Global Markets: A New Macro Strategy

Macroeconomic Arbitrage

Directional and long/short macro trading and investment strategies are based on macroeconomic views. What if we do not have views? What if we do not want to bet on our subjective macro views? We will introduce in this chapter a new macro strategy that we developed, one that is based on detecting objective macroeconomic mispricings in markets: *macroeconomic arbitrage*. This will be the main focus of our book from here on. We will try to shift emphasis from subjective macro views to *objective macro mispricings* in global markets, from directional to long/short and arbitrage. Traditionally in trading, the term *arbitrage* refers to a long/short strategy in which one expects the correction of a certain mispricing in the market of the relation between two assets or of a related market inefficiency: convertible arbitrage, relative value arbitrage, merger arbitrage.

Let us introduce arbitrage strategies in macro trading and investment based on detecting objective macroeconomic mispricings in global markets. A *macroeconomic mispricing* (see Figure 1.1) is an incorrect pricing of macroeconomic variables and indicators and of the relations between these in the prices of related assets and in the relations between them in the markets. This is represented symbolically in Figure 5.1, the diagram of macroeconomic arbitrage. Macroeconomic arbitrage takes advantage of gaps or holes that appear between ratios (spreads) of related assets or groups of assets and ratios of underlying driving macroeconomic variables related to these assets.

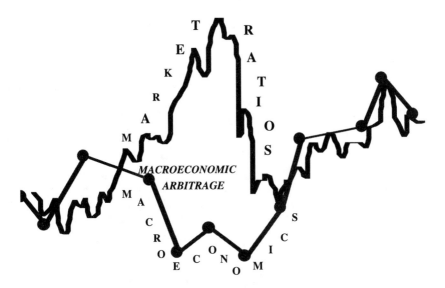

Figure 5.1

Symbolic representation of a new type of macro strategy: Macroeconomic Arbitrage. This new long/short macro strategy was designed by the author to take advantage of macroeconomic mispricings between a spread/ratio of two related assets and the spread/ratio of two underlying related macroeconomic variables or indicators. Macroeconomic arbitrage speculates the divergence gaps between market ratios/spreads and macroeconomic ratios/spreads.

Let us examine in Figure 5.2 the idea of macroeconomic arbitrage in stock markets in more depth. The ratio of two stock indices or related sector indices follows the evolution of the ratio of the two corresponding values of driving macroeconomic variables or economic indicators specific for each of the two chosen indices, assets, or groups of assets. At some stage a divergence gap appears for various reasons, and this constitutes a *macroeconomic arbitrage opportunity*. The closing of this gap is the correction on which one has to bet by buying, in this case, the spread between the two stock indices or assets.

Figure 5.2

The idea of Macroeconomic Arbitrage. Consider a ratio of two assets or two groups of assets (e.g., two stock indices or two sector indices) and the ratio of two corresponding driving macroeconomic variables or of the two specific values of a common driving macroeconomic variable/indicator for the two chosen assets. The two ratios, the market one and the macroeconomic one, track each other until a medium- or short-term divergence appears. After a while a correction takes place, and the two diverging ratios converge to each other.

(Original strategy and figure designed and presented by the author using Datastream database and graphics.)

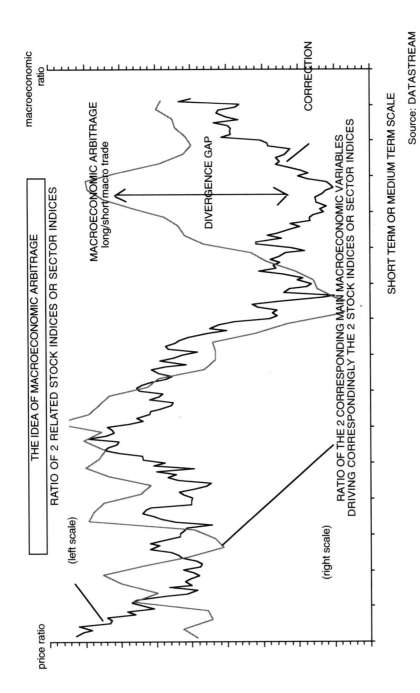

THE IDEA OF MACROECONOMIC ARBITRAGE

RATIO OF 2 RELATED STOCK INDICES OR SECTOR INDICES

price ratio

(left scale)

MACROECONOMIC ARBITRAGE
long/short/macro trade

DIVERGENCE GAP

CORRECTION

macroeconomic
ratio

RATIO OF THE 2 CORRESPONDING MAIN MACROECONOMIC VARIABLES
DRIVING CORRESPONDINGLY THE 2 STOCK INDICES OR SECTOR INDICES

(right scale)

SHORT TERM OR MEDIUM TERM SCALE

Source: DATASTREAM

Figure 5.3

Identifying short-term macroeconomic arbitrage opportunities: the prototype model. A macroeconomic mispricing of a driving macro variable ratio into a related stock index or sector index market ratio is a symmetric divergence gap: one ratio goes up and the other goes down instead of tracking each other or temporarily deviating slightly from each other. It is the clear opposition of directions of movement of the two that increases the probability of future convergence by both ratios reverting back to the convergence/tracking level. The macro trade consists in this case in selling the market ratio (stock indices or sector indices ratio) in expectation that this should revert back to the level at which the initial divergence (mispricing) first appeared. Technical timing of the trade is crucial: the double top in the market ratio indicates the possible beginning of a correction. We can see a new macro arbitrage opportunity just opening at the end of the chart, and again topping is obvious: after four months of tracking and correct macroeconomic pricing, a mispricing appears again in the market ratio.

(Original strategy and figure designed and presented by the author using Datastream database and graphics.)

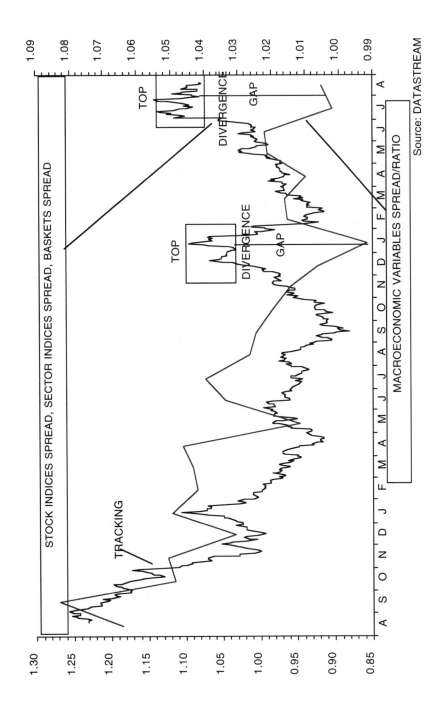

Source: DATASTREAM

A *macroeconomic mispricing gap* is a symmetric divergence of the market price ratio from the macroeconomic ratio. Macroeconomic arbitrage focuses thus on mispricings of macroeconomic relations in the corresponding relations between asset prices in global markets. The prototype model of this new type of long/short macro strategy is shown in Figure 5.3. After periods of close tracking and other periods of move in coincidental directions, the ratio between the two assets moves sharply upward in clear opposition to the underlying macroeconomic variables ratio, which moves sharply downward. This creates the first divergence gap shown in Figure 5.3. This is a clear opportunity to sell the ratio (spread) of the two assets (stock indices, sector indices) because the correction of such a symmetric gap is highly likely to occur through a fall in the asset ratio (spread) at some later stage combined with a recovery and a rally in the macroeconomic variables ratio. The basic rule of macroeconomic arbitrage is to look for sharp divergences with clear opposition of direction because this ensures a higher probability of correction of this mispricing by joint turns in the two ratios toward the equilibrium level before the divergence took place. One can see a second mispricing opening up at the right end of the chart.

Technical timing in macro arbitrage is discussed in Chapter 9, but let us preliminarily note here that the forming of the two highlighted tops in Figure 5.3 are important consolidation signals to follow when triggering such a trade: the break of these tops is the entry point in a macro arbitrage trade. The gaps at the left end of the chart are not mispricing gaps because the directions of the macro ratio and market ratio are the same.

Macroeconomic arbitrage is a new type of long/short macro strategy. As an investment strategy, it can be implemented as an overweight/underweight rebalancing of an investment portfolio in case the mispricing gap has a long- or medium-term time horizon as shown in Figure 5.2. The crucial thing about macro arbitrage is that it is noncorrelated with the market (see Chapter 12), making this strategy valuable in difficult market periods (without trend and pattern).

Chapter **6**

Comparison between Macroeconomic Arbitrage, Directional Macro, and Long/Short Macro Strategies

How does macroeconomic arbitrage compare to long/short macro and directional macro strategies? Long/short macro strategies (see Chapter 4) consist of betting on the direction of a spread between two assets using views on a macroeconomic variable that drives the spread (ratio). The difference between the traditional long/short macro and macroeconomic arbitrage is simply the difference between subjective macro views and objective macro mispricings, as shown by comparing Figure 5.3 with Figure 6.1. The same spread (ratio) of two assets (stock indices, sector indices, and so on) is shown in both these figures, but in Figure 6.1 a longer time period is shown and one underlying explanatory macroeconomic variable is considered rather than a ratio of two macro variables (one for each asset), as in Figure 5.3. The strategy (what to buy and what to sell) can be explicitly read from the chart in Figure 5.3 after identifying the first mispricing gap (which corresponds to January 1997 in Figure 6.1). Figure 6.1 has one big invisible element: the macro views on the future or at least on the next shift in the underlying macroeconomic variable or indicator. It is this subjective element that shows what the trade is as opposed to macro arbitrage in which the trade can be objectively picked up from the chart directly. The difference between macro arbitrage and long/short macro in general is similar to the difference between objective science and subjective art.

Directional trading and investment are not always based on subjective views. As Figure 6.2 explains, macroeconomic arbitrage can lead to directional trades (buy or sell only) when mispricing gaps are detected between the price of an asset or a group of assets and an underlying driving macro variable. In the case of the first divergence gap that appears in Figure 6.2, one buys the asset under consideration given the high probability of the asset price having to correct upward in order to converge back to the driving macro factor that it otherwise tracks.

Figure 6.1

Comparison between long/short macro based on macro views and macro arbitrage based on macroeconomic mispricings: subjective macro versus objective macro. This figure shows the same ratio of two stock indices or sector indices as does Figure 5.3 considered over a longer time horizon and against one driving underlying macro variable or indicator. In a long/short macro trade, it is the view on the underlying macro variable (here shown to be a bearish view) that triggers the selling of the market ratio (spread). Rather than *objectively* identifying a macro mispricing in markets, as in macro arbitrage, in a long/short macro trade it is a *subjective* macro view or expectation (based nevertheless on an in-depth analysis) that triggers the spread (ratio) sell decision.

(Original strategy and figure designed and presented by the author using Datastream database and graphics.)

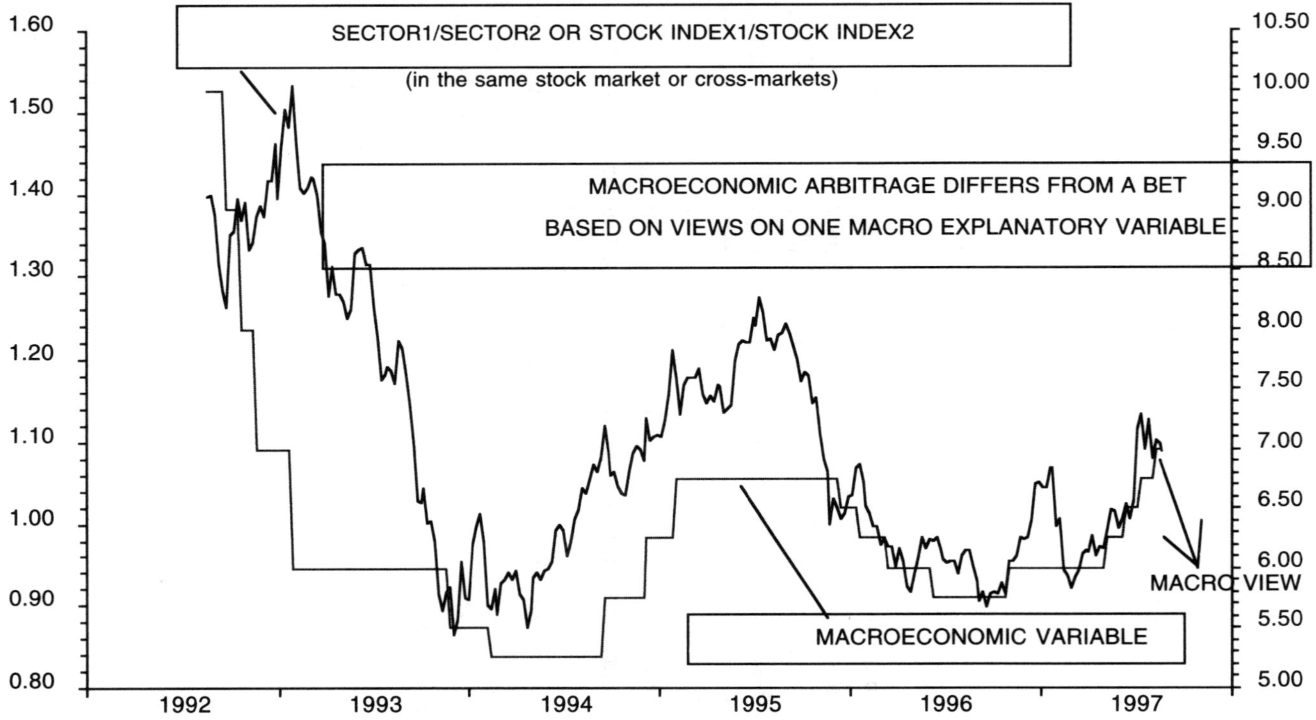

SECTOR1/SECTOR2 OR STOCK INDEX1/STOCK INDEX2
(in the same stock market or cross-markets)
MACROECONOMIC ARBITRAGE DIFFERS FROM A BET
BASED ON VIEWS ON ONE MACRO EXPLANATORY VARIABLE
MACROECONOMIC VARIABLE
MACRO VIEW
1.60
1.50
1.40
1.30
1.20
1.10
1.00
0.90
0.80
10.50
10.00
9.50
9.00
8.50
8.00
7.50
7.00
6.50
6.00
5.50
5.00
1992
1993
1994
1995
1996
1997

Source: DATASTREAM

Figure 6.2

Directional macroeconomic arbitrage. One asset or basket of assets (stock index, sector index, basket) tracks a macroeconomic variable or indicator until a mispricing gap appears and the two diverge from each other only to converge back at a later stage. We have here one asset versus one macro variable and not a spread (ratio) of assets versus a ratio of macro indicators or variables. The way to take advantage of the first mispricing divergence gap indicated in the figure is to buy the asset after it emerges out of the bottom of the gap on expectation of a rally to converge back to the underlying macro indicator. If there is an instrument representing the macro variable (for example, interest rate futures for interest rates) then a nondirectional long/short trade can be initiated by buying the asset and selling the future instrument representative of the macro variable.

(Original strategy and figure designed and presented by the author using Datastream database and graphics.)

Source: DATASTREAM

Chapter 7

Macroeconomic Arbitrage Based on Retail Sales Mispricings in Markets

Macroeconomic Arbitrage: Retail Sales

A typical macro trading and investment strategy for stock markets is generally based on macro views on inflation, interest rates, and exchange rates, and it is often implemented by buying or selling stock index futures. What about the other macroeconomic variables, like retail sales, gross domestic product (GDP), and new orders? If they are taken in consideration, it is only as auxiliary variables to determine potential inflation and thus to lead to views on interest rates

The depth of macroeconomics has so much more to offer to macro traders and investors. Retail sales, for example, can on its own be the subject of a macroeconomic arbitrage strategy. Rather than trying to form views on inflation based on retail sales, one can check whether retail sales is correctly priced in the market. Let us go one level down, from the stock index market level to the sector level. The market level and the individual stock level are the most preferred levels by macro investors who apply their views by either trading futures or stock picking. The sector level in between these other preferred levels very often gets ignored by macro investors.

We can see in Figure 7.1 that in the United Kingdom food and general retail sales volumes control the relation between the two corresponding sectors of the stock market: food retailer stocks and general nonspecialized retailer stocks, provided the margins of these two sectors and their dynamics are comparable. Figure 7.1 shows over four years the close relation (tracking) between the macroeconomics ratio of food retail sales volume and general retail sales volume on one side and the market price ratio of food retailer stocks and general retailer stocks on the other side. Periods of tracking are interrupted by clear divergences such as in January 1997 or the last quarter of 1997 when the market ratio of the two sectors moved upward while the macro ratio pointed in clear opposition downward. These are clear symmetric divergences, and they signal a macroeconomic mispricing due to some temporary shift of attention on micro issues or on other secondary economic variables and indicators. Whatever happened, if the margins of the two sectors stay the same, higher general retail sales volumes should reflect in general retailer stocks outperforming the food retailer stocks. Gaps like the one at the beginning of 1997 do not represent obvious mispricings because the ratio of retail sales volumes ultimately moved down in the same direction with the market price ratio of the two sectors.

Using the same sector indices as in Figure 7.1, Figure 7.2 shows in depth the macroeconomic arbitrage strategy "long UK general retailer stocks/short UK food retailer stocks," which takes advantage of the mispricing created in the last quarter of 1996 between the relation of retail sales volumes and the relation of the corresponding sectors of the UK stock market. By January 1997 it was clear that there was a divergence gap signaling a strong mispricing (explained probably by interest-rate-hike fears). What was needed was a pattern of topping and consolidation of the outperformance rally of food retailer stocks over general retailer stocks. As soon as the highlighted double top appears, it is time to pull the trigger expecting a correction downward of the sector indices ratio toward the equilibrium, horizontal, central line of the mispricing gap, back to the level at which the initial mispricing divergence started. This correction amounts to an 8 percent (very conservative estimate) outperformance of general retailers over food retailers in three weeks. Implementation of the trade is done by selecting the five most liquid, high-market-cap names in each of the two sectors and by building two tracking baskets for the two observed sector indices. Another mispricing gap is just opening at the

Figure 7.1

Retail sales mispricings in the UK food retailer stocks/general retailer stocks price ratio (spread). The ratio of sector indices UK food retailers sector index/UK general retailers sector index is driven by an underlying macroeconomic variables ratio: UK food retail sales volume/UK general retail sales volume, provided margins in the two sectors are comparable. Periods of correct pricing and tracking are interrupted by clear divergences, such as at the end of 1996 or the middle and last quarter of 1997. After a while these mispricing gaps close, and the stock market sector ratio converges to the macroeconomic ratio. Not every gap in between the two ratios is a mispricing gap: at the beginning of 1996 the two ratios moved in the same direction (down) but with some delay, creating the illusion of a mispricing. We can see a mispricing gap "in action" opening at the end of 1997.

The following sector indices were used:

UK food retailers sector index	UK general retailers sector index
ASDA	Laura Ashley
Kwik Save	Argos
Morrison	Boots
Safeway	Dixons
Sainsbury	Great Universal Stores
Somerfield	Kingfisher
Tesco	Marks & Spencer
	Next
and others	and others

(Original strategy and figure designed and presented by the author using Datastream database and graphics.)

FOOD RETAILERS/GENERAL RETAILERS

SECTOR INDEX PRICE RATIO

SALES VOLUME FOOD RETAILERS

SALES VOLUME GENERAL RETAILERS

MISPRICING GAP

MACROECONOMIC ARBITRAGES

6/2/98

1.09
1.08
1.07
1.06
1.05
1.04
1.03
1.02
1.01
1.00
0.99
0.98

1.30
1.25
1.20
1.15
1.10
1.05
1.00
0.95
0.90
0.85

1995
1996
1997
1998

Source: DATASTREAM

Figure 7.2

Macroeconomic arbitrage based on retail sales mispricing in the food retailer stocks/general retailer stocks ratio (spread). In December 1996 the UK food retailer stocks/general retailer stocks ratio deviates from the underlying ratio of retail sales volumes in the two sectors. Although the dynamics of margins in the two sectors was comparable at that time, the volume of general retail sales were outperforming the food retail sales volume, while in the stock market prices of food retailers were outperforming general retailers. During January 1997 this mispricing stops progressing further and enters a consolidation phase, clearly topping (clear double top in the food retailers sector index/general retailers sector index ratio). At end of January 1997 this double top breaks, and this is the right moment to initiate a macroeconomic arbitrage trade by selling short UK food retail stocks and buying general retail stocks. This is equivalent to selling the stock index ratio (spread) in the figure in expectation of it going down to converge back to the macroeconomic fundamentals of retail sales at the middle level of the mispricing gap created, back at the level where the initial mispricing started to develop. In three weeks this trade generated 8 percent gross return.

The following sector indices were used:

UK food retailers sector index	*UK general retailers sector index*
ASDA	Laura Ashley
Kwik Save	Argos
Morrison	Boots
Safeway	Dixons
Sainsbury	Great Universal Stores
Somerfield	Kingfisher
Tesco	Marks & Spencer
	Next
and others	and others

(Original strategy and figure designed and presented by the author using Datastream database and graphics.)

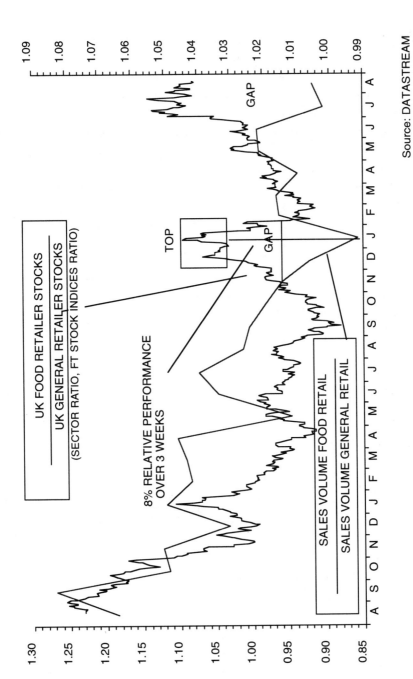

UK FOOD RETAILER STOCKS

UK GENERAL RETAILER STOCKS

(SECTOR RATIO, FT STOCK INDICES RATIO)

8% RELATIVE PERFORMANCE
OVER 3 WEEKS

TOP

GAP

GAP

SALES VOLUME FOOD RETAIL

SALES VOLUME GENERAL RETAIL

Source: DATASTREAM

♦ 65 ♦

right end of the chart, but as we will see in Chapter 9, a careful technical examination of this opportunity will show major obstacles in the way of a smooth correction.

We can conclude that while using macroeconomic information, not only is macro arbitrage nondirectional but, as can be seen from the example of UK food retailers/general retailers, this strategy can lead to a market-neutral strategy if the sensitivities with respect to the market (betas) of the long basket of general retailers and short basket of food retailers are matched. Macro can be *market neutral*, not just directional!

Chapter 8

Causes of Macroeconomic Mispricings in Markets and Tackling Secondary Macroeconomic Variables in Trades

What is the cause of these mispricings of macroeconomic relational information in the corresponding relations between assets in markets? One major cause is that whereas an asset might be directly driven and explained by a macroeconomic variable, the same asset can be the object of an almost mechanical reaction to shifts in another secondary macroeconomic variable. Consider again the food retailers/general retailers macroeconomic arbitrage, using the same sector indices but this time displayed with UK base interest rates as in Figure 8.1. We can clearly see that interest rates are responsible for the long-term general trend and appear as a sort of envelope of the sector indices price ratio, whereas, as expected, retail sales volume is the fine tuning that leads to shaping patterns and swings in the balance between food retailer stocks and general retailer stocks. Interest rate fears generate automatic defensive switches in market, like moving out of general retailer stocks into food retailer stocks. However, if these fears are not confirmed and the general retail sales volumes continue to be higher than food retail sales volumes, the initial psychological overreaction has to be corrected back to the macro reality of these sectors, as in January 1997. The major cause of macro mispricings is a shift of attention to economic variables and indicators that are not directly and immediately related to the performance of the assets under consideration. The other obvious cause is individual stock stories; for example, merger talks between two companies in the

UK food retail sector in mid-1997 caused the new mispricing gap opening up at the right end of the chart in Figure 7.2.

One approach to secondary macroeconomic variables in macro arbitrage is based on checking their anticipation by the futures market before triggering the actual long/short trade. For example, three months short sterling interest rate futures are displayed together with the base rates in Figure 8.1. In January 1997 when the macro mispricing gap was ready for correction, one can see that on the background of unchanged UK base rates, short sterling futures (in fact, 100 minus the price of the short sterling interest rate future contract, which is a direct measure of the anticipated rates in three months) started pointing downward rather than sharply upward at the end of 1996. This sign of fading subjective fears plus the technical signs of consolidation rather than further expansion of the mispricing gap (double top formed in the ratio in January) were the trigger to put on the trade.

Figure 8.1

Causes of macroeconomic mispricings and tackling secondary macroeconomic variables in macro arbitrage. As we saw in Figures 7.1 and 7.2, UK food and general retail sales are the variables influencing the relation between UK food retailer stocks and general retailer stocks, provided margin dynamics are comparable in the two sectors. However there is another macro variable, short-term interest rate, that dictates the general medium- and long-term direction of the UK food retailers/general retailers ratio: retail sales gives the fine tuning whereas interest rates give the envelope (interest rates are like an envelope for the food retailer stocks/general retailer stocks price ratio). Investors switch away from general retailers to food retailers (perceived as more defensive) when there are fears of rising interest rates. However, if the real economic reality shows better general retail sales than food retail sales, the interest rate fears create a macroeconomic mispricing, sometimes pushing the market price ratio of the two sectors in a direction opposite to the underlying retail sales volume reality. Fears versus reality—that is how mispricings appear.

The market expectation of interest rates can be read in interest rate futures (three-month short sterling futures in this case): While the base rate in the United Kingdom stayed unchanged from the end of 1996 until mid-1997, short sterling futures clearly indicate interest-rate-hike fears associated with inflationary fears in the last quarter of 1996. This led to a defensive switch into food retailers although general retailers had better sales volume due to "windfall money" received by consumers after the demutualization of some building societies. As can be seen in the March 1997 short sterling futures, these fears disappear as 1997 starts, and this triggers the correction in food retailers/general retailers back in favor of general retailers, at which the reality of retail sales kept pointing for a while.

The same sector indices were used as in Figures 7.1 and 7.2.

(Original strategy and figure designed and presented by the author using Datastream database and graphics.)

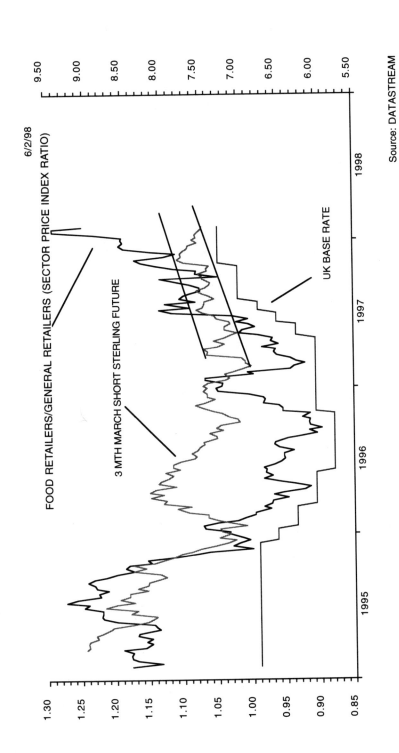

FOOD RETAILERS/GENERAL RETAILERS (SECTOR PRICE INDEX RATIO)

6/2/98

3 MTH MARCH SHORT STERLING FUTURE

UK BASE RATE

Source: DATASTREAM

♦ 71 ♦

Chapter **9**

The Importance of
Technical Timing
in Macro Arbitrage

Our new approach to trading macroeconomic mispricings is a *fundamental-technical-quantitative unified approach* (see Figure 9.1). Macroeconomic fundamentals lead us to creating correspondences between pairs of assets or groups of assets and pairs of macroeconomic variables that decisively influence the former, for example, food retail sector/general retail sector and food retail sales volume/general retail sales volume. Technicals allow us to detect mispricings and to plan the macro arbitrage trade based on these mispricings. As we saw earlier, technical timing is crucial in deciding if there is enough in the trade and when to initiate it. Macroeconomic fundamentals play another role in explaining these technically detected mispricings by bringing in perhaps other macro variables and indicators.

Ultimately, quantitative analysis is used to measure and to quantify relations between assets and underlying macroeconomic fundamentals, leading to quantitative detection of macro mispricings. This book is trying to be as visual as possible, and it is for this reason that we will not get into quantitative details too often. However, we will see, for example, in Chapter 17 how quantitative methods are used to measure sensitivity to Asian stockmarkets and to point to a mispricing of the Asian crisis in the Finnish/Swedish stock indices spread. Interpreting spreads (ratios) of assets or groups of assets as new long/short synthetic assets leads to developing a correlation and volatility analysis of these macroeconomic arbitrage opportunities, such as in Chapters 11 and 12. In Chapter 19, regression analysis will be again used to build a dollar-sensitive basket of French stocks.

Macroeconomics can be combined successfully with technical and statistic analysis in macroeconomic arbitrage trading and investment strategies. Let us look at an example of technical timing analysis in the macroeconomic arbitrage of mispriced representations of food retail sales volume/general retail sales volume macro ratio in the market price ratio food retailers stocks/general retailers stocks explained in Chapter 7.

Figure 7.2 showed how identifying a broken double top in the ratio between the two stock market sectors in January 1997 led to initiating the long/short macro trade. The second clear mispricing gap highlighted in Figure 9.2 in mid-1997 exhibited a similar topping pattern. However, although we have a topping mispricing ready to correct, one can see that if such a mispricing correction were to start, important trend support line 2 might be in the way of our macro arbitrage trade, limiting the extent of the correction. It is not one support line that will get in the way but two: line 1 (given by the level of the previous high in January 1997 before the double top was formed and broken) comes to meet line 2 to form a strong double resistance in the way of our correcting spread. This suggests a limited profit potential in initiating a macro arbitrage trade based on the correction of the mid-1997 mispricing gap in UK food retailers/general retailers. Figure 9.2 shows the accuracy of this technical assessment. Indeed, as soon as the correction hits the level where lines 1 and 2 meet, food retailers start outperforming again, and our stock indices price ratio bounces back up. The mispricing gap was ultimately closed but in a very volatile way that led to big drawdowns in a possible long/short macro arbitrage trade that might have tried to take advantage of this mispricing.

Figure 9.1

Macro arbitrage requires a unified fundamental-technical-quantitative approach. As we will see in Figure 9.2, retail sales volume and interest rate expectations are as important as support trendlines and double tops in identifying a successful macro arbitrage trade.

**MACROECONOMIC ARBITRAGE: TAKING
ADVANTAGE OF MACROECONOMIC
MISPRICINGS**

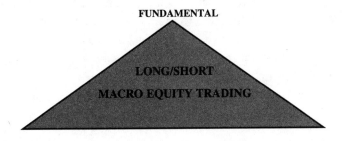

Figure 9.2

The importance of technical timing in macro arbitrage. The technical factors suggested that the second macro arbitrage opportunity in
1997 had very few chances to lead to a profitable long/short macro
trade. Two important support lines came in the way of a meaningful
complete correction in UK food retailers/general retailers: the support
trendline of the ratio during 1997 (line 2) and the horizontal level
line (line 1) of the high of the ratio in January 1997 before the previous macroeconomic mispricing gap started to close. As the correction
starts after mid-1997, the falling ratio simultaneously meets the support lines 1 and 2 (enhanced support) and bounces very strongly back
up to the level from which it started falling, only to come back down
later with renewed strength and to finally penetrate the two intersect-
ing support lines. The first mispricing gap of 1997 had much better
technical conditions, culminating with a clear broken double top signaling the beginning of correction.

The following sector indices were used:

UK food retailers sector index	UK general retailers sector index
ASDA	Laura Ashley
Kwik Save	Argos
Morrison	Boots
Safeway	Dixons
Sainsbury	Great Universal Stores
Somerfield	Kingfisher
Tesco	Marks & Spencer
	Next
and others	and others

(Original strategy and figure designed and presented by the author using
Datastream database and graphics.)

FOOD RETAILERS/GENERAL RETAILERS

SECTOR INDEX PRICE RATIO

SALES VOLUME FOOD RETAILERS

SALES VOLUME GENERAL RETAILERS

MISPRICING GAP

double support 1,2 causes
partial correction in
the second highlighted macro arb

MACROECONOMIC ARBITRAGES

6/2/98

Source: DATASTREAM

♦ 79 ♦

Chapter 10

The Relation between Macro and Micro Fundamentals in Macro Arbitrage

So far, the term *fundamental* was used assuming implicitly that it refers to *macroeconomic fundamentals*. What about fundamental analysis and the fundamentals of stock valuation and earnings? These are the micro fundamentals. The relation between these two levels of fundamentals corresponding to the macro and the micro levels of the market is important in macroeconomic arbitrage trading and investment. This is so first of all because macro arbitrage is trying to fill the gap between macro and micro by focusing on the intermediate sector level. Of course, there are, for example, sector hedge funds, but they focus on a specific sector rather than on the relation between various sectors. The other specific thing about macro arbitrage is the focus on the relations between assets rather than on the individual fundamentals, whether they are macro or micro. An essential prerequisite of macro arbitrage is checking the coincidence of directions between the direction of the ratio of macro fundamentals of the two assets under consideration (or two groups of assets) and the direction of the ratio of micro fundamentals. If both directions coincide and the ratio of the two assets points in an opposite diverging direction, the macro mispricing we identified is not explained by micro fundamentals or, equivalently, is not in conflict with micro fundamentals.

It was this compatibility between macro and micro that was envisaged in Chapter 7 when we repeatedly mentioned that the margins of food retailers and general retailers should be comparable or that their dynamics should be similar because otherwise the macro mispricing we identified has nothing to do with retail sales but is explained by a shift in the balance between the margins of the two sectors. Figure 10.1 illustrates these considerations by comparing in the United Kingdom the ratio of retail sales volumes with the ratio between the earnings of food retailers and general retailers: the former is the macro fundamental we selected to monitor, and the latter is the micro fundamental element. One can see the long term coincidence of the micro and macro trends. In January 1997, during the macro mispricing described in Chapter 7 in UK food retailers/general retailers, the higher general retail sales volume was signaled in advance by higher earnings in the general retail stocks sector than in the food retail stocks sector. In 1995, the macro trend drifted away from the micro trend probably because of, among other reasons, lower margins in the food sector shaken by recent price cuts ("price war") which led to lower earnings. Although volumes were bigger in food retailers, lower margins led to lower earnings in food retailers than in general retailers. If, for example, a macro mispricing would have been identified in this period during 1995, it would have been a pseudo (false) macro mispricing explained in fact by hidden micro valuation factors (margins, earnings). The macro and micro trends can be different, but a successful real macro arbitrage opportunity requires the coincidence of the two trends allowing for possible lagging.

Stocks will always be traded predominantly for micro reasons (value traders watching earnings and price/earnings [P/E] ratios, growth traders watching earnings growth or momentum, etc.). There are mispricings, invisible at the micro level, that require one to pull back and aggregate at the macro level at which the strategy we developed identifies new macroeconomic mispricings. Any such successful macro trading strategy should ensure that the new macroeconomic relations it tracks do not disagree very much with the micro fundamental relations. It is not the identity of the two that is needed (then one can be replaced by the other) but their noncontradiction.

The other obvious relation between macro and micro is that additional micro selection or stock picking can enhance the profit of a

Figure 10.1

The relation between macro fundamentals (retail sales) and micro fundamentals (earnings). It is important to have no contradiction between the *macro* trend (based on retail sales ratio) and the *micro* trend (based on the earnings ratio) for the sector index ratio UK food retailers/UK general retailers indicates. This will eliminate the possibility of some hidden micro valuation reason for a macro mispricing. In 1995, while the micro trend in earnings ratio was in favor of general retailers, the macro trend in retail sales was in favor of food retailers. A clear wide gap was created, suggesting that margins in the food sector were suffering more while trying to recover after recent price cuts.

The following sector indices were used:

UK food retailers sector index	UK general retailers sector index
ASDA	Laura Ashley
Kwik Save	Argos
Morrison	Boots
Safeway	Dixons
Sainsbury	Great Universal Stores
Somerfield	Kingfisher
Tesco	Marks & Spencer
	Next
and others	and others

(Original strategy and figure designed and presented by the author using Datastream database and graphics.)

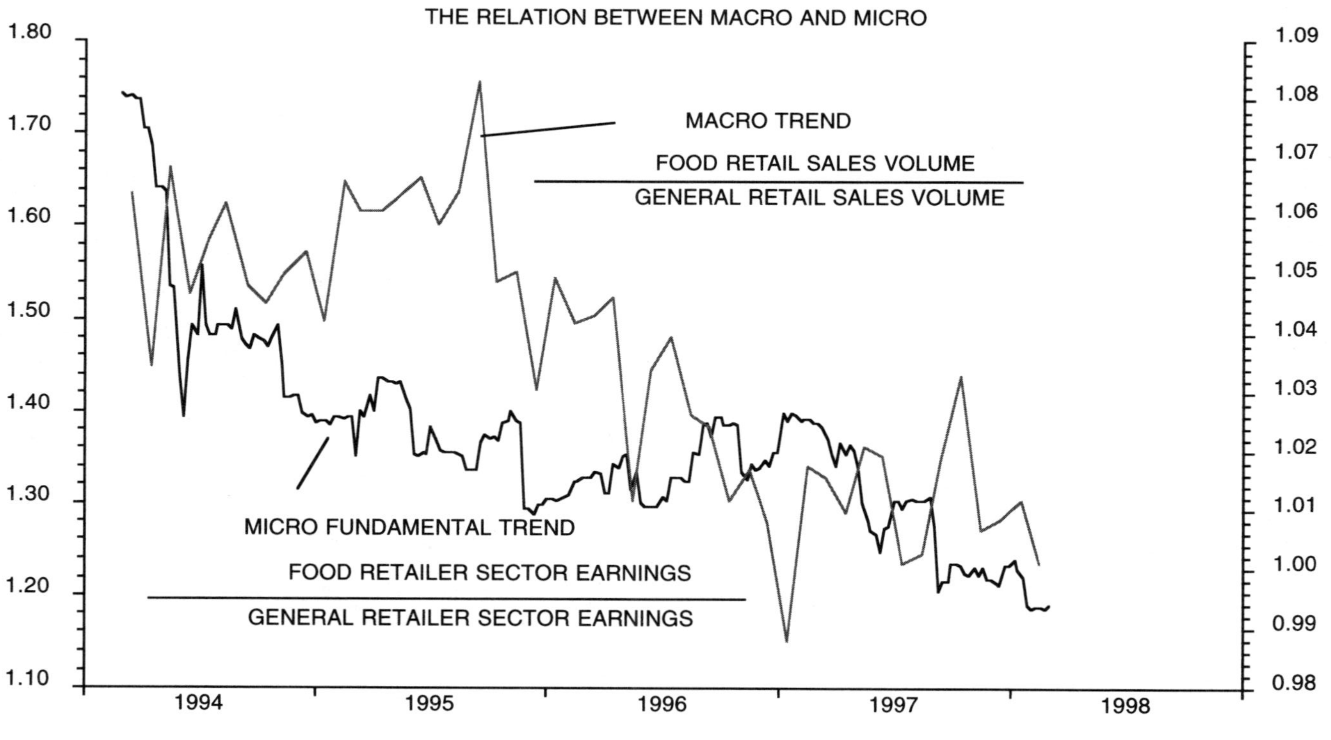

THE RELATION BETWEEN MACRO AND MICRO
MACRO TREND
FOOD RETAIL SALES VOLUME
GENERAL RETAIL SALES VOLUME
MICRO FUNDAMENTAL TREND
FOOD RETAILER SECTOR EARNINGS
GENERAL RETAILER SECTOR EARNINGS
1.80
1.70
1.60
1.50
1.40
1.30
1.20
1.10
1.09
1.08
1.07
1.06
1.05
1.04
1.03
1.02
1.01
1.00
0.99
0.98
1994
1995
1996
1997
1998

Source: DATASTREAM

strategy based on macroeconomic information. In a bullish dollar-sensitive-stocks strategy in Europe, one buys exporters that are dollar sensitive. Picking dollar-sensitive stocks that have, say, great earnings momentum is an example of how macro works in a joint strategy with micro.

Chapter 11

Volatility of Macro Arbitrage Strategies versus Relative Value Strategies

One of the two main reasons for long/short macro strategies is to have a lower volatility as compared to directional macro bets while keeping reasonably high returns (see Figure 2.2). Of course, the other reason is to provide additional unexploited sources of returns. Let us see if this really turns out to be the case.

One of the strategies perceived to have lower volatility than directional trading is *equity relative value arbitrage*. This is a long/short equity strategy involving two stocks that very often are the two listed parent companies of the same unlisted joint holding company. Probably the most famous example is Royal Dutch Shell Group in which Royal Dutch Petroleum in the Netherlands has 60 percent interest and Shell Transport in the United Kingdom has 40 percent interest (the dividends of Royal Dutch Shell Group are distributed in a 60/40 ratio to the two parent companies listed in the United Kingdom and the Netherlands). Going long one of the parent companies and short the other is perceived to be a conservative, low-risk, very well established, equity relative value strategy involving the same underlying fundamentals of the unlisted joint holding. A similar example is the unlisted ABB Group in which ABB AB in Sweden and ABB AG in Switzerland each have 50 percent interest as listed parent companies. ABB AB/ABB AG and Royal Dutch/Shell are probably the most popular equity relative value arbitrages or switches, known equally in Europe and the United States because Royal Dutch is listed in the United

States as ADR and it is in the Standard & Poor's (S&P) 500. A macro trader will never even look at these switches and a relative value trader will never look at macro strategies because they feel it is too risky to have long/short positions of different companies, rather than having the same underlying company, involved.

Let us try to compare the volatility of the United Kingdom food retailers/general retailers long/short macro arbitrage strategy with that of the two most famous equity relative value arbitrage switches ABB AB/ABB AG and Royal Dutch/Shell. In the comparisons for Figures 11.1 and 11.2, annualized 20 days rolling volatility was used. Calculating the average volatility over the two-year time period shows that the average volatility of a macro arbitrage trade is very similar to the volatility of equity relative value strategies (the ratio UK food retailers/general retailers returns has an average volatility of 15 percent, while ABB AB/ABB AG has 16 percent volatility and Royal Dutch/Shell has 13 percent).

So we managed to create a new strategy based on macroeconomic information, which, contrary to the general perception that macro is high volatility and directional, is a long/short strategy having the same volatility as a relative value arbitrage, which is perceived as nonrisky and safe. The importance of this will be shown in the next chapter after analyzing the correlation of this new macro strategy with directional and relative value strategies. It will be shown that macro arbitrage can be added in a small weight to a market-neutral or relative-value portfolio of strategies, and the effect will be to increase overall returns of the new portfolio while changing the overall risk level very little.

Figure 11.1

Volatility of a macro arbitrage strategy versus the volatility of a relative value strategy: first example. We compare the 20-day annualized rolling volatility for the returns of UK food retailers/UK general retailers macro arbitrage and for ABB AB (Sweden)/ABB AG (Switzerland) classical equity relative value pair arbitrage. ABB AB (listed in Stockholm) and ABB AG (listed in Zurich) are the Swedish and Swiss holding companies of the same underlying unlisted ABB Group (relative value equity pair). Averages of the volatilities of the two totally different strategies are very close. We have thus engineered a macro strategy that, as opposed to the traditional macro volatile strategies, has almost the same volatility as a relative value strategy.

The following sector indices were used:

UK food retailers sector index	UK general retailers sector index
ASDA	Laura Ashley
Kwik Save	Argos
Morrison	Boots
Safeway	Dixons
Sainsbury	Great Universal Stores
Somerfield	Kingfisher
Tesco	Marks & Spencer
	Next
and others	and others

(Original strategy and figure designed and presented by the author using Datastream database and graphics.)

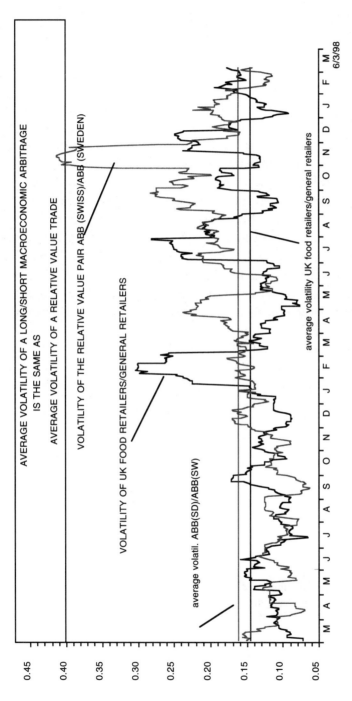

AVERAGE VOLATILITY OF A LONG/SHORT MACROECONOMIC ARBITRAGE
IS THE SAME AS

AVERAGE VOLATILITY OF A RELATIVE VALUE TRADE

VOLATILITY OF THE RELATIVE VALUE PAIR ABB (SWISS)/ABB (SWEDEN)

VOLATILITY OF UK FOOD RETAILERS/GENERAL RETAILERS

average volatil. ABB(SD)/ABB(SW)

average volatility UK food retailers/general retailers

Source: DATASTREAM

6/3/98

Figure 11.2

Volatility of a macro arbitrage strategy versus the volatility of a relative value strategy: second example. We compare the 20-day annualized rolling volatility for the returns of UK food retailers/UK general retailers macro arbitrage and for Royal Dutch/Shell classical equity relative value pair arbitrage. Royal Dutch (listed in Amsterdam and in New York) and Shell (listed in London) are the Dutch and UK parents of the same underlying Royal Dutch Shell company. Averages of the volatilities of the two totally different strategies are very close. We have thus engineered a macro strategy that, as opposed to the traditional macro volatile strategies, has almost the same volatility as a relative value strategy.

The following sector indices were used:

UK food retailers sector index	UK general retailers sector index
ASDA	Laura Ashley
Kwik Save	Argos
Morrison	Boots
Safeway	Dixons
Sainsbury	Great Universal Stores
Somerfield	Kingfisher
Tesco	Marks & Spencer
	Next
and others	and others

(Original strategy and figure designed and presented by the author using Datastream database and graphics.)

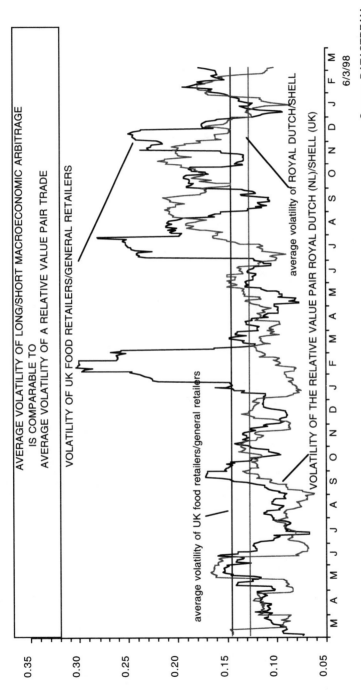

AVERAGE VOLATILITY OF LONG/SHORT MACROECONOMIC ARBITRAGE IS COMPARABLE TO AVERAGE VOLATILITY OF A RELATIVE VALUE PAIR TRADE

VOLATILITY OF UK FOOD RETAILERS/GENERAL RETAILERS

average volatility of UK food retailers/general retailers

average volatility of ROYAL DUTCH/SHELL

VOLATILITY OF THE RELATIVE VALUE PAIR ROYAL DUTCH (NL)/SHELL (UK)

Source: DATASTREAM

6/3/98

Chapter 12

Macro Arbitrage Is Uncorrelated to Directional and Relative Value Strategies

Macro Arbitrage: Uncorrelated Strategy

The main motivation behind any new type of strategy is first of all to provide an additional uncorrelated source of returns. The typical example is provided by relative value and market neutral strategies, which proliferated due to them having very low correlation with the market. This way, when markets fall or consolidate and directional buy-only strategies lose money, market neutral and relative value strategies provide an uncorrelated source of positive returns (the new backup "alphas"). Macroeconomic arbitrage discovers new types of (macroeconomic) mispricings in global markets and takes advantage of the mispricings' future correction through a long/short macro trade. So far, great, we have a new long/short macro strategy, but its value will be even greater if we can show it is uncorrelated with the returns of directional macro strategies as well as with the returns of other strategies, for instance, equity relative value arbitrage. Then not only have new mispricings been detected, but the strategy speculating them is also a source of totally new uncorrelated returns so that when directional macro and relative value stragegies lose money, macro arbitrage can be a good hedge by generating positive returns (alphas). From the logic of macroeconomic arbitrage method it is intuitively clear that as it makes no use of market direction information, returns of directional macro should be in principle uncorrelated with returns of macro arbitrage strategies. Let us check on a specific example to show that this is really the case. Figure 12.1 shows 30 days rolling correlation between returns of the UK stock index FTSE 100 (the asset frequently used in directional macro UK equity trades implemented by buying FTSE 100 futures) and the returns of UK food retailers/UK general retailers long/short macro spread. The average correlation for the two-year time period shown in the figure is –0.05 (uncorrelated). Let us have an even deeper look at the January–February 1997 time window when the macro arbitrage trade described in Chapter 7 was triggered. During that time window correlation averaged an insignificant 0.1. In Figure 12.1, the macro arbitrage strategy has the merit of generating a new type of returns (alphas) uncorrelated with the macro directional returns.

What about equity relative value strategies? Figure 12.2 shows 30 days rolling correlation between the returns of the equity relative value arbitrage discussed in Chapter 11, Royal Dutch/Shell Transport, and the returns of UK food retailers/UK general retailers. As expected intuitively, the average correlation over the two-year period displayed in the figure is 0 (uncorrelated). Again, during the January–February 1997 time window of the macro arbitrage trade discussed in Chapter 7, the average correlation was an insignificant –0.1.

The importance of finding a new type of long/short macro strategy that is uncorrelated with other strategies and that, like all macro strategies, has a higher return than the average nondirectional strategies can be seen from the following calculations. Assume a portfolio P of nondirectional, market neutral, relative value trading and investment strategies having overall return R and variance V. Let P' be the new portfolio obtained by allocating a small 10 percent (0.1) weight to the macro arbitrage strategy (having say return RM and variance VM) and a weight of 90 percent (0.9) to the mix of strategies in P. The return and variance of P', denoted by R' and V', are given by the following classical formulas of portfolio theory:

$$R' = 0.1*RMA + 0.9*R$$

$$V' = 0.01*VM + 0.81*V + 2*corr(M,P)*0.1*0.9*sqrt(VM)*sqrt(V)$$

where "$corr(M, P)$" denotes the correlation between the returns of the initial market neutral, relative value portfolio P and the returns of the

Figure 12.1

Macro arbitrage is uncorrelated to directional macro strategies. Thirty days rolling correlation between the returns of UK food retailers/UK general retailers and the returns of FTSE 100 (market) shows an average of −0.05 (uncorrelated). In particular, during the January–February 1997 time window corresponding to the macro arbitrage opportunity shown in Figure 7.1 and discussed in Figure 7.2, we can see that the correlation again averaged a small 0.1.

The following sector indices were used:

UK food retailers sector index	UK general retailers sector index
ASDA	Laura Ashley
Kwik Save	Argos
Morrison	Boots
Safeway	Dixons
Sainsbury	Great Universal Stores
Somerfield	Kingfisher
Tesco	Marks & Spencer
	Next
and others	and others

(Original strategy and figure designed and presented by the author using Datastream database and graphics.)

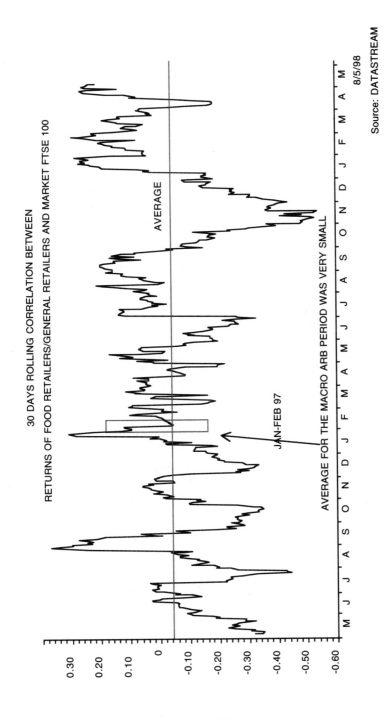

30 DAYS ROLLING CORRELATION BETWEEN
RETURNS OF FOOD RETAILERS/GENERAL RETAILERS AND MARKET FTSE 100

AVERAGE

JAN-FEB 97

AVERAGE FOR THE MACRO ARB PERIOD WAS VERY SMALL

Source: DATASTREAM

8/5/98

Figure 12.2

Macro arbitrage is uncorrelated to relative value strategies. Thirty days rolling correlation between the returns of UK food retailers/general retailers and the returns of Royal Dutch/Shell shows an average of 0 (uncorrelated). Royal Dutch (listed in Amsterdam and in New York) and Shell (listed in London) are the Dutch and UK parents of the same underlying Royal Dutch Shell company (equity relative value pair). In particular, during the January–February 1997 time window corresponding to the macro arbitrage opportunity shown in Figure 7.1 and discussed in Figure 7.2, we can see that the correlation again averaged a small –0.1.

The following sector indices were used:

UK food retailers sector index	UK general retailers sector index
ASDA	Laura Ashley
Kwik Save	Argos
Morrison	Boots
Safeway	Dixons
Sainsbury	Great Universal Stores
Somerfield	Kingfisher
Tesco	Marks & Spencer
	Next
and others	and others

(Original strategy and figure designed and presented by the author using Datastream database and graphics.)

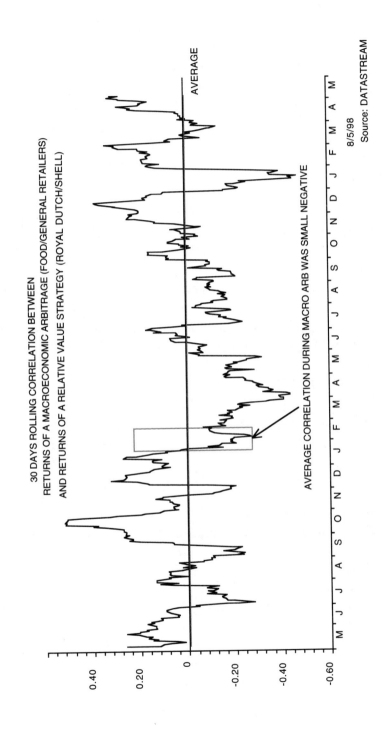

30 DAYS ROLLING CORRELATION BETWEEN
RETURNS OF A MACROECONOMIC ARBITRAGE (FOOD/GENERAL RETAILERS)
AND RETURNS OF A RELATIVE VALUE STRATEGY (ROYAL DUTCH/SHELL)

AVERAGE

AVERAGE CORRELATION DURING MACRO ARB WAS SMALL NEGATIVE

8/5/98

Source: DATASTREAM

macro arbitrage strategy subportfolio M, and "sqrt" denotes the square root. As macro arbitrage is uncorrelated with other strategies the last term in the sum defining V' will be very small and can be neglected. Because only a small dose (weight) of macro arbitrage was mixed with the initial portfolio P, the square of this weight appearing in the formula of V' is even smaller (0.01) and can be ignored compared with the other term left $0.81*V$. We get an approximate estimate for the risk (variance) of the new portfolio P' very close to the variance V of P, the initial low-risk portfolio. However, if the returns of the macro arbitrage strategy subportfolio M are higher than the average relative value and market neutral strategies, they will be transparent even after multiplication by the small weight 0.1 (it is the square of this weight that becomes so small that we ignored the term it multiplies in V'). We can conclude that due to the uncorrelated new high returns created by macro arbitrage, in a *fund of funds* portfolio of strategies P', macro arbitrage boosts the overall returns of P' while affecting its risk very little, provided only a small weight (typically no more than 15 to 20 percent maximum) of a macro arbitrage long/short portfolio is added to a relative value and market neutral low-risk portfolio P.

This has implications in managing a fund of funds. This is a fund invested in various hedge funds that focus on different, ideally uncorrelated strategies. A fund of funds is very well modeled by our portfolio P' having differently weighted strategies. Macro arbitrage can often be implemented as a market neutral long/short strategy by matching the betas of the long sector (basket) and the short sector (basket). (See the remark at the end of Chapter 7.) "Injecting" macro arbitrage with a small weight of 0 to 20 percent maximum in a long/short market neutral, relative value, fund of funds portfolio improves returns while affecting the risk very little. Of course, all these theoretical considerations are assuming implicitly that the relative value, the market neutral, and the macro arbitrage strategies are all successful and generate positive returns. These thoughts should be taken in a qualitative effect analysis sense as they have no predictive power! We understand now why we should always search for new strategies, provided they generate uncorrelated new alphas (returns).

Chapter 13

Macro Arbitrage Trading and Investment Based on Gross Domestic Product (GDP) Mispricings in Global Markets

G ross *Domestic Product* (GDP) is the barometer of an economy, expressing synthetically in one number the total output of goods and services. *GDP growth* indicates how an economy expands or contracts, and it is one of several overall macroeconomic reflections of the corporate earnings growth. It is therefore not surprising that the relation between the GDPs of two countries (expressed as a macroeconomic ratio of the two GDPs' growth) is accurately priced in the relation between the two stock market indices of the two countries (expressed as a market price ratio of the two stock indices). This is a *long-term macroeconomic relation* priced in the relation between the markets over a long time horizon.

Figure 13.1 shows how the ratio of the Dutch and the German stock indices correctly prices in the macroeconomic ratio of the two countries' GDP growth over a 15-year time horizon. Since 1990, Dutch stock index EOE has constantly outperformed German stock index DAX, creating a clear upward outperformance trend line on expectations of stronger and stronger Dutch GDP growth relative to German GDP growth, which translated into expectations of higher corporate earnings in Holland relative to Germany. The recent breaking of this trend is in part explained by Germany's recovery from the recessionary period created by the costs of integrating the former East Germany with the former West Germany after the fall of the Berlin wall. (*Recession* is often defined as two consecutive quarters of negative GDP growth.)

The only macro mispricing gap between the GDPs' growth ratio and the two stock indices' ratio is shown in the 1986–1987 period where twice EOE outperformed DAX significantly, despite the Dutch GDP slowdown relative to Germany. Figure 13.1 was an example of a good long Netherlands/short Germany macro investment strategy for the 1990s (overweight Netherlands/underweight Germany) based on views and expectations of faster Dutch growth. The relation between the two stock markets is very strong: Dutch chemical stocks react to news and results in German chemical stocks, and this sector has an important weight in both EOE and DAX. Financials play a major role in both stock indices as well and are highly correlated. Although it is a cross-market stock index ratio, EOE/DAX has almost no influence from the Dutch Guilder/German Deutschmark FX rate, which hardly fluctuates particularly in the recent pre-European Monetary Union years.

A similar example of how the GDP ratio is correctly priced in the stock indices ratio of two related stock markets is in Figure 4.6 where among others one can see the relation between Italian GDP growth/Spanish GDP growth on one side and Italian stock index/Spanish stock index ratio on the other side. This example is particularly instructive in the context of the discussion started in Chapter 8 on tackling several macroeconomic variables in long/short macro and macro arbitrage trades. Figure 4.6 shows the interaction between GDP and interest rates as macroeconomic variables that are compared to decide the future direction of the Italian/Spanish stock indices spread. GDP is not alone in a macro trade; interest rates are there as well if there is a specific story like the Euroconvergence story. GDP has to be the dominant macro variable at a certain moment to justify triggering a macro trade using GDP as main argument. Figure 4.6 illustrates the existence of alternating periods in which macro variables compete for the central role: although it was clear that Italian rates had to fall more than the Spanish ones, the better Spanish GDP growth (pointing to better corporate earnings growth prospects) became the dominating macro variable over interest rates. However, as Italian GDP growth catches up to Spanish GDP growth, at least on paper, the focus will be moving to interest rates where 100 basis points (bps), or 1 percent differential

Figure 13.1

Correct macroeconomic pricing of the long-term relation between Dutch and German GDP growth into the spread (ratio) between the Dutch stock market index EOE and the German stock market index DAX. For nine years, the Dutch stock market constantly outperformed (clear outperformance trend) the German stock market, reflecting the expectation of higher macroeconomic growth in the Netherlands and thus higher corporate earnings growth. The recent breaking of this trend is a reflection of a historical shift in the balance between the Dutch and the German GDP growth in favor of the latter. Long term, the market ratio of the two stock indices tracks, with few mispricings, the macro ratio of the growth of the two respective GDPs. Perhaps one exception from this correct macroeconomic pricing in the relation between the two markets was in 1986 and 1987, when a slowing Dutch growth relative to German growth took a while to be matched in the relation between the two corresponding stock indices. The attraction of the EOE/DAX ratio is that although it is a cross-market ratio, the exchange rate exposure Dutch Guilder/German Mark (Deutschmark) is minimal because this exchange rate fluctuates very little, particularly over the last years due to European Monetary Union convergence expectations. The two stock markets also have similar concentrations of chemicals and financials—chemicals in the Netherlands follow chemicals in Germany, and so on. Finally, this figure was a good example of a long/short macro investment strategy for the 1990s because it suggests overweighting the Netherlands and underweighting Germany, based on views suggesting Dutch growth should be faster than German growth.

(Original strategy and figure designed and presented by the author using Datastream database and graphics.)

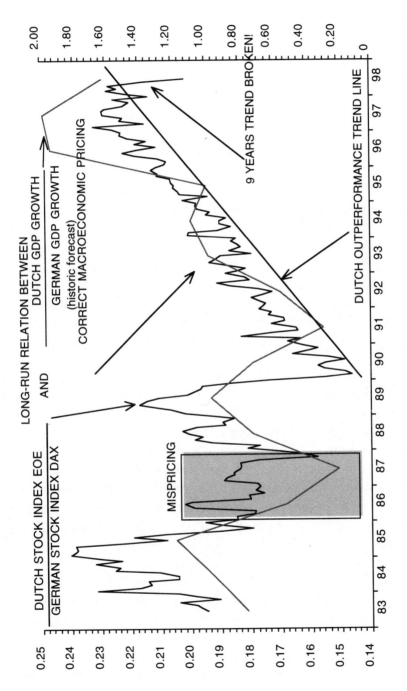

Source: DATASTREAM

has to go by January 1999. Bear in mind the worries about the sustainability of the Italian growth.

GDP, as a macroeconomic variable, influences equally the macro level of the market (stock index level), the micro stock level (stocks sensitive to the GDP "economic cycle" are called *cyclical*; stocks not sensitive to GDP growth cycles are called *defensive*) and as we plan to show next, the intermediate sector level.

In both the United States and the United Kingdom, the balance between the very cyclical construction stocks sector and the less cyclical building materials stocks sector is dictated by the strength of the economy and in particular by GDP growth. Take first the United Kingdom (Figure 13.2): whenever there is a recession, construction slows dramatically, while the sale of building materials slows less because maintenance repairs, for example, have a more permanent, defensive nature; the recovery of the economy with GDP increasing positive growth stimulates construction stocks proportionally with new constructions, industrial expansions, and property demand. Although this relation is very intuitive, we spent a lot of time measuring the sensitivities of the returns of these two sectors with respect to GDP by using regression analysis to decide quantitatively that one sector is more cyclical than the other.

So what happened in 1994 and 1995 when a clear macroeconomic mispricing gap appeared between GDP growth and the ratio UK construction sector/UK building sector, which otherwise has a clear long-term relation with GDP growth that is accurately priced in the two sectors market price ratio? One of the worst recession periods in the modern history of the United Kingdom ended in 1993 (GDP growth came from negative –3 percent to positive 2 percent after sterling left the European Exchange Rate Mechanism). Although there was clear recovery on paper, the confidence of both business and consumers was still very weak, as if they could not yet believe in the recovery: there was a lack of courage to build and expand and a weak property market. Construction stocks continued to underperform building materials stocks. Technical analysis gave an important signal at the end of 1995: the construction sector/building materials sector ratio hit the low level seen at the bottom of the recession. With GDP growing stronger and stronger, no matter how great the lack of confidence after a hard recession, this lack could not lead to levels of underperformance below the recession level. At this crucial low support level with the help of increasing confidence, a clear bullish head-and-shoulders base develops in a few months, leading to the expected outperformance of construction stocks over building material stocks. This was a two-year macro arbitrage investment opportunity long construction sector/short building materials sector (overweight construction/underweight building materials stocks). At the end of 1996 one of the widest mispricing gaps of GDP in UK markets closed. GDP acts as a *leading indicator*, meaning there is a lag before the market reacts to major turns in GDP growth, and this is why one needs to shift forward the GDP in any macroeconomics/markets overlay chart.

It is reassuring to find in the United States the same long-term relation between GDP and the *cyclical sector spread* home building stocks/building materials stocks shown in Figure 13.3. This long-run macroeconomics/market relation is not as precise as in the United Kingdom because it is restricted to one particular type of construction (home building), leaving aside the very important component of industrial construction. However, the first quarter of 1997 saw the bottoming out of a wide-range macroeconomic mispricing gap between the GDP and the market sector ratio. The highlighted broken double bottom (B) gave the signal for a macro arbitrage trade long home building stocks/short building materials stocks, which in one month led to a gross profit of 8 percent.

Figure 13.2

Macro arbitrage investment strategy based on GDP mispricing in UK stock market: construction stocks versus building materials stocks. The ratio (spread) UK construction stocks/UK building material stocks is a cyclical ratio tracking the driving leading GDP (one-year, forward-shifted, quarterly-percentage-change series). A serious mispricing appears in the early 1990s at the exit from one of the most serious recessions that the United Kingdom has experienced. During recessions, new construction stagnates while maintenance repairs and modifications keep the demand for building materials going, therefore leading to building materials stocks outperforming construction stocks. While the GDP quarterly growth recovers in positive territory, the lack of consumer and business/industry confidence continues to affect construction. As the recovery becomes stronger and stronger, new construction projects are finally initiated, triggering the correction and the closure of the mispricing gap between the construction stocks/building materials stocks ratio and the quarterly GDP during the period 1996–1997. This mispricing was a clear opportunity for a one- or two-year macro arbitrage investment opportunity: overweight UK construction stocks/underweight UK building materials stocks. Note again the importance of technical factors other than macroeconomics in a macro investment strategy: the bottoming of the ratio construction sector/building materials sector started when the low level of the recession was hit. This acted as strong support for a rebound because it was clear that in a strong recovery, construction stocks should not underperform building material stocks more than they had during the recession.

The following sector indices were used:

UK construction sector index	UK building material sector index
AMEC	BCI
Ashtead	Caradon
Barratt	Hepworth
McAlpine	Pilkington
Mowlem	RMC
Taylor Woodrow	Rugby
Wimpey	Tarmac
and others	and others

(Original strategy and figure designed and presented by the author using Datastream database and graphics.)

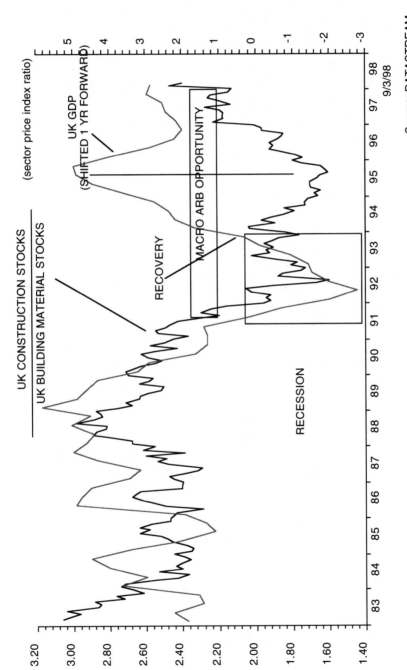

Source: DATASTREAM

9/3/98

UK CONSTRUCTION STOCKS
─────────────────────────────
UK BUILDING MATERIAL STOCKS

(sector price index ratio)

UK GDP
(SHIFTED 1 YR FORWARD)

RECOVERY

MACRO ARB OPPORTUNITY

RECESSION

Figure 13.3

Macro arbitrage investment strategy based on GDP mispricing in the U.S. stock market: home building sector versus building materials sector. The same relation as in Figure 13.1 can be seen in the U.S. stock market where the ratio (spread) home building stocks/building materials stocks follows on long-term scale the quarterly percentage change in the U.S. GDP. A clear divergence appears between the two at the end of 1996. The economy is booming, but fears of the Federal Reserve Bank again using interest rate hikes to slow down the economy keeps home building stocks behind building materials stocks. As it becomes more and more clear that we have a noninflationary growth and as the GDP growth itself slows down, home building confidence pushes home building stocks up and closes down a wide mispricing gap. Note again that a double bottom in the home building/building materials stocks ratio gives a reliable technical signal for the beginning of the correction. This mispricing was a good opportunity for a six-month to one-year time horizon macro arbitrage investment strategy: overweight home building stocks/underweight building materials stocks. Alternatively, a long/short (medium-term) macro arbitrage trading strategy indicated long home building sector/short building materials sector. Even if the stocks used in this example are far less liquid than their UK counterparts in Figure 13.1, it is instructive to find the same type of mispricings and strategies based on their correction in both the United Kingdom and the United States.

The following sector indices were used:

S&P 500 home building sector index	S&P 500 building materials sector index
Centex	Armstrong-World
Fleetwood	Masco
Kaufman & Broad	Owens-Corning
Pulte	

(Original strategy and figure designed and presented by the author using Datastream database and graphics.)

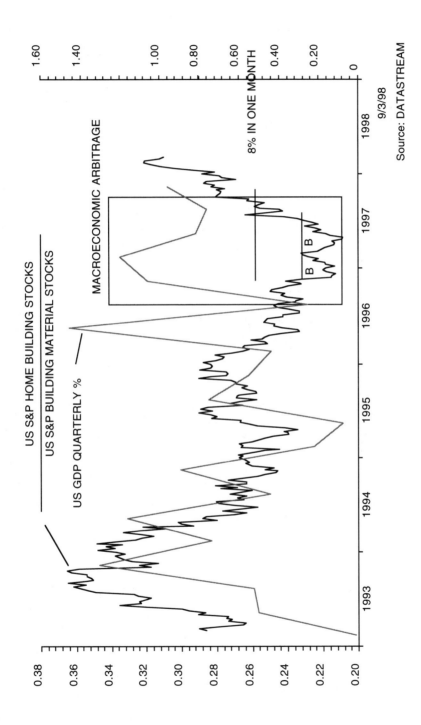

US S&P HOME BUILDING STOCKS

US S&P BUILDING MATERIAL STOCKS

US GDP QUARTERLY %

MACROECONOMIC ARBITRAGE

8% IN ONE MONTH

1993   1994   1995   1996   1997   1998

9/3/98

Source: DATASTREAM

0.38 0.36 0.34 0.32 0.30 0.28 0.26 0.24 0.22 0.20

1.60 1.40 1.00 0.80 0.60 0.40 0.20 0

Chapter 14

Macro Arbitrage Based on Interest Rates Mispricing in Global Markets

Macro Arbitrage: Interest Rates

How views and expectations on interest rates and interest rate spreads between two markets can be used to generate an interest-rate-based directional macro strategy and an interest-rate-based long/short macro strategy was shown in Chapters 1 and 4, respectively. In both cases short-term interest rates were used (one month, three months). From now on, we can assume that we do not want to bet on our views on interest rates because either we do not have any views or we do not feel confident in our views. What is the alternative? First of all, let us make the most of interest rates by looking at both short-term and long-term rates (10-year benchmark bond yields). The difference between the short- and long-term rates is called the *yield curve steepness*. In Figure 14.1 the spread (ratio) between Spanish banks and Spanish utilities tracks closely the Spanish yield curve steepness historic series defined as the difference between 10-year benchmark bond (bonos) yield and 1-week MIBOR short-term rate. This close tracking is not just a coincidence! Banks are interest-rate-sensitive stocks that benefit from falls in short-term rates because their business-lending margins increase this way, whereas utilities invest traditionally in long bonds and government benchmark bonds. Then it is clear why banks outperform utilities when the yield curve steepens and vice versa when the yield curve flattens, as can be seen in Figure 14.1 over a four-year time horizon.

Let us find next the macroeconomic arbitrage opportunity by looking for a clear macro mispricing. In order to visualize clearly a macro mispricing gap, it is very important that one moves up and down along the time axis. Figure 14.1 gives a clear picture of the relation between yield curve steepness and the Spanish banks/ Spanish utilities stocks ratio. By moving forward the four-year time window, we can clearly capture in Figure 14.2 the mispricing gap from 1996: it is wide, symmetric, and clearly divergent. So for it to correct, both parts will have to do their own bit of homework. For us it is the Spanish banks/ Spanish utilities bit that mattered as soon as the head-and-shoulders base formation at mid-1996 signaled consolidation or the beginning of correction: long Spanish banks/short Spanish utilities. Of course, it is important to ensure that rates are the main driving engine, and not any ongoing restructuring process, privatization, or major difference between the growth of the two sectors acting to widen the mispricing gap further. Also, as the gap opening in mid-1997 shows, technical factors can sometimes contribute to widening gaps until a target is reached, and then, due to refocus on macro fundamentals, correction can finally take place.

So why is there such a huge mispricing gap opening wider and wider in 1997 despite the clear flattening of the yield curve and the lack of any fabulous mergers in Spanish banks that might have explained the outperformance? Of course, the repeated tranches of privatization of Endesa, the largest Spanish utility, and the Euroconvergence leading to short rates falling and banks outperforming are part of the explanation. Figure 14.3 brings an additional reason: the technical reason. A big double bottom was formed in the Spanish banks/Spanish utilities market price ratio by the end of the first quarter of 1997—the double bottom of the large underperformance fall of banks versus utilities in 1995 as investors switched into utilities as bond proxies. The target of this major bullish base formation was back at the top at the beginning of 1995. Only after reaching that target level of such a powerful, impressive, one-year-long bottom formation will the probability of any correction of this mispricing increase. And indeed, have a look again at Figure 14.2 (the future) after watching Figure 14.3 (the past with its technical prediction for the near future): Spanish banks/Spanish

Figure 14.1

Relation between interest rates (long yields minus short-term-rates differential) and the banks/utilities sector price ratio. The yield curve steepness (10-year Spanish "bonos" benchmark yield minus one-week MIBOR rate) is an underlying driving factor for the ratio between Spanish banks (favored by falling short-term rates) and Spanish electric utilities (invested like all utilities in long bonds). The more the yield curve steepens, the more banks outperform electric utilities, assuming no major restructuring potential and growth differences between the two.

The following sector indices were used:

Spanish banks sector index	*Spanish utilities sector index*
Argentaria	Endesa
BBV	FECSA
BCH	Gas y Electricidad
Popular	Hidrocantabrico
Santander	Iberdrola
Banesto	Sevillana
Bankinter	Union Fenosa
and others	and others

(Original strategy and figure designed and presented by the author using Datastream database and graphics.)

SPANISH BANKS
——————————
SPANISH UTILITIES

V.S.

10-YEAR YIELD – 1-WEEK MIBOR RATE
(YIELD CURVE STEEPNESS SPREAD)

27/6/97

4.50
4.00
3.50
3.00
2.50
2.00
1.50
1.00
0.50
0

1994   1995   1996   1997

0.56
0.54
0.52
0.50
0.48
0.46
0.44
0.42
0.40
0.38

Source: DATASTREAM

♦ 119 ♦

Figure 14.2

Macroeconomic arbitrage based on interest rates mispricings in the Spanish banks/Spanish utilities sector price ratio. In the middle of 1996 a clear macroeconomic mispricing gap appeared between the long/short interest rate differential and the ratio Spanish banks/Spanish utilities. This was a macroeconomic arbitrage opportunity to buy Spanish banks and sell short Spanish utilities (buying the spread) for 10 percent gross profit over three months. We can see an unusually wide mispricing opening in the middle of 1997 due to the "EMU factor" (see Figures 3.1–3.4): on expectations of Spain joining the EMU in 1999, investors switched heavily into financials, which are interest-rate sensitive, and out of bonds into equities (utilities are associated with long bonds).

We used the following sector indices:

Spanish banks sector index	Spanish utilities sector index
Argentaria	Endesa
BBV	FECSA
BCH	Gas y Electricidad
Popular	Hidrocantabrico
Santander	Iberdrola
Banesto	Sevillana
Bankinter	Union Fenosa
and others	and others

(Original strategy and figure designed and presented by the author using Datastream database and graphics.)

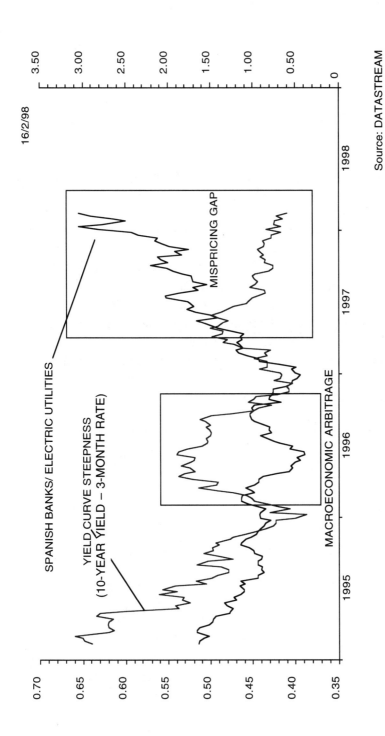

Source: DATASTREAM

16/2/98

Figure 14.3

Technical factors explaining the large macroeconomic mispricing starting in the middle of 1997 due to expectations that Spain will join the EMU in 1999. Why is the macroeconomic mispricing gap from Figure 14.2 so wide, so ongoing without correction? The EMU factor triggered it as explained in Figure 14.2 and led to the breaking of a very bullish, powerful, one-year-wide double-bottom base in the banks/utilities ratio. Its target and new resistance was the top level achieved in 1995 before utilities started outperforming the banks big time as investors switched out of equities into bonds, perceiving utilities as bond proxies. Again, as in Figure 9.2, technicals and EMU-related fundamentals warned that this mispricing would be hard to arbitrage.

The following sector indices were used:

Spanish banks sector index	*Spanish utilities sector index*
Argentaria	Endesa
BBV	FECSA
BCH	Gas y Electricidad
Popular	Hidrocantabrico
Santander	Iberdrola
Banesto	Sevillana
Bankinter	Union Fenosa
and others	and others

(Original strategy and figure designed and presented by the author using Datastream database and graphics.)

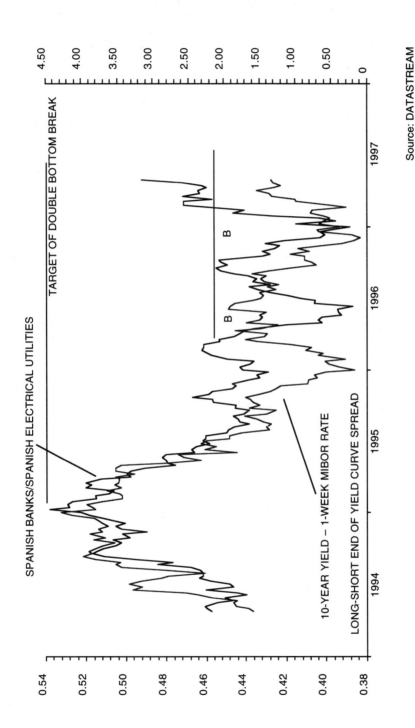

SPANISH BANKS/SPANISH ELECTRICAL UTILITIES

TARGET OF DOUBLE BOTTOM BREAK

B

B

10-YEAR YIELD – 1-WEEK MIBOR RATE

LONG-SHORT END OF YIELD CURVE SPREAD

Source: DATASTREAM

utilities stopped rallying and started consolidating in the form of what appears to be the beginning of a double top. Probably as soon as Endesa's last tranche of privatization is finished and Spanish interest-rate cuts hit the bottom ahead of the 1999 European Monetary Union (EMU), this wide mispricing gap will close, unless bank mergers start contaminating the quiet Spanish corporate scene.

Chapter 15

Macro Arbitrage of Consumer Expenditure Mispricings in Global Markets

Macro Arbitrage: Consumer Expenditure

Consumer spending among various goods affects the performance of the sectors producing these goods and in the end should determine the stock market valuation of these sectors. We have a path from consumer demand to sector stock index price that indicates that the relations among goods-producing sectors in stock markets can be decisively influenced by the balance between the corresponding flows of consumer demand and spending. In the United Kingdom, the ratio between the alcoholic beverages manufacturers and the food manufacturers sector stock indices has a long-term, or long-run, relation with the balance between consumer expenditure on beer (the main alcoholic beverage in the United Kingdom) and consumer expenditure on food. Let us call it the "drink and eat spread" (Figure 15.1).

In Figure 15.2, we magnify the time axis in order to better capture a clear mispricing divergence gap in 1996, which gets lost in the big picture of Figure 15.1. This mispricing gap hits a major two-year support line shown in the figure (the historic low level for the previous four years for the alcoholic beverage manufacturers stocks/food manufacturers stocks market ratio). A bullish base is soon developed after bouncing off the support. At that stage a clear macroeconomic arbitrage opportunity existed, and, indeed, the way in which the mispricing was corrected and the gap closed can be seen.

Macro Arbitrage: Consumer Expenditure

Consumer expenditure and retail sales are very much related to each other. Whereas *retail sales* involves goods sold in retail stores, *consumer expenditure* also includes the restaurants, bars, and caterers that make a big difference particularly for food and drink. We always limit ourselves to related sectors, such as drink/food, cars/car parts, construction/building materials. This is important in order to factor out any stories specific to one sector (and irrelevant to the other) that might explain the shift in the balance between the two sectors rather than the shift being explained by any macroeconomic ratio of variables or indicators.

Figure 15.1

Long-term relation between a sector index ratio and a driving macroeconomic variables ratio: consumer expenditure long-term pricing in the stockmarket. UK alcoholic beverages stocks/UK food manufacturers stocks versus beer consumer expenditure/food consumer expenditure where we used the following sector indices:

UK alcoholic beverages manufacturers sector index	UK food manufacturers sector index
Allied Domecq	Albert Fisher
Bulmer	British Foods
Diageo	Cadbury
Glenmorangie	Dalgety
Highland Distilleries	Tate & Lyle
Mathew Clark	Unilever
	United Biscuits
	and others

(Original strategy and figure designed and presented by the author using Datastream database and graphics.)

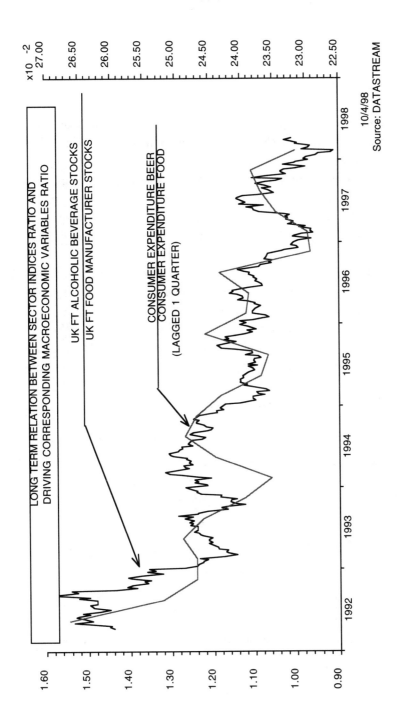

LONG TERM RELATION BETWEEN SECTOR INDICES RATIO AND
DRIVING CORRESPONDING MACROECONOMIC VARIABLES RATIO

UK FT ALCOHOLIC BEVERAGE STOCKS
UK FT FOOD MANUFACTURER STOCKS

CONSUMER EXPENDITURE BEER
CONSUMER EXPENDITURE FOOD
(LAGGED 1 QUARTER)

10/4/98
Source: DATASTREAM

Figure 15.2

Macroeconomic arbitrage based on consumer expenditure mispricing in the alcoholic beverage/food manufacturers sector price ratio. The time scale is crucial in detecting macro investment or trading opportunities. By considering a five-year time window (not six years as in Figure 15.1), we can detect more clearly divergence gaps due to macro mispricings like the one appearing in mid-1996 when although consumer spending on beer was greater than consumer spending on food, the stock market had priced this proven long-term relation the reversed way—with food manufacturers stocks outperforming alcoholic beverage manufacturers stocks. This was a clear macro arbitrage opportunity with significant technical factors: the mispricing gap paused on a one-year, very significant support. A clear base was formed in the sector ratio, which, when it was broken, gave the starting signal for a macro arbitrage short-term trade: long alcoholic beverage manufacturers stocks/short food manufacturers stocks.

The following sector indices were used:

UK alcoholic beverages manufacturers sector index	UK food manufacturers sector index
Allied Domecq	Albert Fisher
Bulmer	British Foods
Diageo	Cadbury
Glenmorangie	Dalgety
Highland Distilleries	Tate & Lyle
Mathew Clark	Unilever
	United Biscuits
	and others

(Original strategy and figure designed and presented by the author using Datastream database and graphics.)

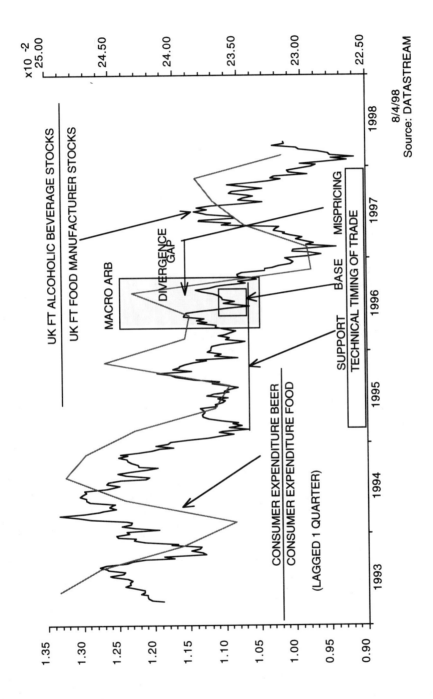

Chapter 16

Macro Arbitrage of Manufacturing Shipments Mispricings in Global Markets

Macro Arbitrage: Manufacturing Shipments

I n the United States, shipments of goods together with inventories
and orders give a very accurate transversal description of the state
of the manufacturing sector: demand-driven orders act on supply-
determined inventories, and this interaction leads to shipments (sales).
Shipments can be pictured as the middle link in this three-stage chain
of the manufacturing sector, giving an indication as to the balance/
imbalance of inventories and to the supply/demand pattern of the
sector. Of course, fast production cycles, such as in the nondurable goods
manufacturing subsector, lead to shipments being often the same as
orders.

There is a long-run relation between the economic ratio computers shipments/semiconductors components shipments and the relative
performance of the two corresponding sectors in the stock market as
measured by the market ratio computer hardware manufacturing stocks/
semiconductors stocks (Figure 16.1). Shipments is a good manufacturing sector activity indicator, and it is not surprising that it should be
observably priced in the market together with other economic variables and indicators. The market ratio follows with higher volatility a
six-month, moving average, smoothed economic ratio, which indicates
the medium-term path to be followed next. Because of being such an
intimate economic activity indicator, shipments are often a volatile
economic series requiring some form of *smoothing* (for example, moving averages) to highlight major trends on long-term perspectives, like

the one shown in Figure 16.1 (10 years). The end of 1995 saw the opening of a several-months-long mispricing that was a macroeconomic arbitrage opportunity for a long semiconductor stocks/short computer hardware stocks four-month trade with an approximate 15 percent correction confirmed potential.

Figure 16.1

**Macroeconomic arbitrage investment based on the long-term rela-
tion between manufacturing shipments and the sector price ratio U.S.
computer hardware stocks/semiconductor stocks.** Provided demand
and margins do not differ too much, the ratio computer hardware stocks/
semiconductor stocks is very much driven by manufacturing shipments.
It is a long-term relation that can be better seen on a 10-year time
window. Clear divergences appear very rarely, such as at the end of
1995: that was an opportunity for a macro arbitrage investment that
could have been implemented as long/short or overweight/underweight.

The following sector indices were used:

U.S. S&P 500 semiconductor sector index	U.S. S&P 500 Hardware sector index
Advanced Micro Devices	Apple Computers
Intel	Compaq Computers
LSI Logic	Data General
Micron	DELL Computers
National Semiconductors	Digital Equipment
Texas Instruments	Hewlett-Packard
	IBM
	Silicon Graphics
	Sun Microsystems

(Original strategy and figure designed and presented by the author using
Datastream database and graphics.)

MACROECONOMIC ARBITRAGE IN LONG TERM PERSPECTIVE

S&P COMPUTER HARDWARE STOCKS

S&P SEMICONDUCTORS STOCKS

MANUFACTURERS' SHIPMENTS OF COMPUTERS

MANUFACTURERS' SHIPMENTS OF SEMICONDUCTORS
(6 MONTHS MOVING AVERAGE OF 1MTH LAGGED DATA)

MACRO ARB OPPORTUNITY
15-20% RETURN OVER 4 MONTHS

DIVERGENCE

Source: DATASTREAM

Chapter 17

Mispricings of Asian Crisis Effects on Global Markets: When Macro Events Trigger Subliminal Market Relations

The Macro Event

The Asian crisis that started in the second half of 1997 will remain as a landmark in stock market history, together with the October 1987 crash. The Asian crisis differed in that it was not just the market dynamics of supply, demand, and ultimately liquidity that caused it but a deep economic crisis based on excessive indebtedness and a slowing growth that failed to back this debt. Growth in Asia slowed because of decreasing exports and decreasing earnings from exports as, for example, the demand for and the yen earnings from Asian exports in Japan were affected by the recently unprecedented yen weakness. There is still debate on the causes of this crisis, but one specific feature that played a role in the spread of the Asian financial ills is the strong pattern of interconnected export/import bilateral flows among the countries in the Asia Pacific zone combined with the strong ties each country has with Japan. Once any piece of the Asian web suffers, these bilateral import/export interconnected flows ensure that the suffering spreads all over! That was the explanation for the domino effect—crises being triggered one after another. Of course it showed first in currencies because they are the immediate barometers of economic health. As opposed to the crash of October 1987 or to the liquidity crisis of 1994 (after the U.S. Federal Reserve Bank surprisingly hiked interest rates), financial markets supply/demand mechanisms were not the engines but just the reflectors of an economic explanatory mechanism. Definitely, the Asian crisis was not caused by currency speculation but by a high indebtedness not matched by equally high revenue-generating exports.

Global financial markets tried immediately to assess the impact of Asia on other markets like the United States and Europe. It was exports and loans to Asia that were used as Asian exposure criteria. The contribution to gross domestic product (GDP) of total exports to Asia was a way to assess the potential slowdown of the GDP growth effect that Asia might have on U.S. and European economies.

Correct Pricing of the Macro Event, Moving Bottom Up from the Micro (Stock) Level of the Market to the Sector Level

Rather than starting at the top stock market index or sector level, this time we will start at the bottom. Relations between individual stocks (micro level) quickly and correctly priced in the Asian exposure effect. In France, the main French retailer stocks, Carrefour and Promodes, dominate the French retail sector to the extent that although there is no cross-holding or any other form of structural corporate connection between the two (actually they are competitors), the two stocks are often associated in long/short equity trading strategies of the switch type. Carrefour is internationally diversified with significant Asian exposure, whereas Promodes is more domestically oriented. So the switch Carrefour/Promodes is often a switch between strength abroad and domestic strength in the retail sector. Figure 17.1 shows an example of correct pricing of the Asian crisis impact at the bottom micro level (relations between stocks). Due to its Asian exposure, Carrefour dramatically underperformed Promodes, paralleling the fall of Asian stock markets when the crisis was full-blown in the second half of 1997. Over the period from October 1997 to March 1998, Carrefour/Promodes ratio moved identically with the overall Asia ex-Japan regional stock index (in US $).

Another example of correct pricing of the Asian markets at the micro (bottom) level is the Philips/Polygram switch. This is a real switch because Philips, the consumer electronics giant, owned three-quarters of Polygram, thus having a dominant share in the music-entertainment business of Polygram. In fact, Philips/Polygram is a *relative value pair* because there is a strong underlying corporate structure relation. As this is being written, Philips is selling this significant stake to Seagram, who is bidding for Polygram. But let us go back to October 1997 (it is always an October!) when the Asian crisis became a reality fully acknowledged by the fall in financial markets. We show in Figure 17.2 how the fall and the base formation (head-and-shoulders look alike) in the global Asia ex-Japan stock index was carbon-copied in the stock price ratio Philips/Polygram, although this switch had a much more limited reaction to the two major falls in Asia in October and January. The reason for Philips/Polygram so accurately pricing in the Asian crisis is that Polygram was perceived as the more defensive component. The Philips consumer electronics business was very much dependent on the demand from Asia, as was the business of all the U.S. computer hardware and semiconductor companies. One reason for the limited damage Asia did to the Philips/Polygram price ratio was the bad performance of Polygram's music business, corresponding to the difficulties of this sector worldwide in 1997 for causes other than Asia. The other more important reason was that not only was Philips exporting to Asia but it was also assembling consumer electronics in Asia. The drastic weakening of the Asian currency meant lower production costs and thus higher productivity. This effect partially hedged the expected weakening of the Asian demand for Philips products.

What we learned from these examples is that it was easy to assess the micro impact of the Asian crisis—the impact at the bottom, individual-stock level. Now let us move from top to bottom, from micro to macro, and see how the impact on relations between individual stocks was correctly or incorrectly aggregated in an impact on the relations between sectors and, further up, in the relations between markets. German car manufacturers were perceived to have a bigger exposure (that is, exports) to Asia than the French car manufacturers. Rather than looking at the ratio German car stocks/French car stocks, which also will have incorporated as a subcomponent the overall local mar-

ket influence (that is, German DAX stock index and French CAC 40
stock index influences on German car stocks and French car stocks,
respectively), we eliminated these local market influences so that we
can compare the pure sector factors rather than sector and local market factors taken together. We did this by comparing the ratio

German cars sector index/German DAX stock index

on one side with the ratio

French cars sector index/French CAC 40 stock index

on the other side (see Figure 17.3). Each of the two ratios represents
the relative performance of the respective sector relative to its local
market. In this way Figure 17.3 illustrates the impact of Asia on the
two sectors rather than including the impact on the overall local French
and German market. For trading purposes such a cross-market sector
relative performance ratio as the one just described is implemented by
the following equivalent position:

Long French car stocks/Short CAC 40 futures

Short German car stocks/Long DAX futures

Figure 17.3 shows the correct pricing of the Asian crisis in this relative sector performance ratio, which tracked closely the regional Asia
ex-Japan overall stock index starting from July 1997.

All the examples seen so far point to an interesting theoretical
remark. There are some relations in markets, let us call them *subliminal relations*, that are hidden and forgotten under normal circumstances,
although the information pointing to them is there and available. A
certain macro event acts as a trigger refocusing the market on those
subliminal relations as if the market suddenly remembered them. Who
cared about Carrefour's Asian exposure before Asia became a major
issue?

Figure 17.1

Correct pricing of the Asian crisis in a micro equity spread (pair): Carrefour/Promodes (French retailers pair) versus Asia ex-Japan region stock index. Carrefour has more significant Asian exposure than Promodes, which is more domestically oriented. So when Asia entered the serious crisis period, Carrefour underperformed Promodes, and the ratio between the two tracked identically the Asia ex-Japan index.

(Original strategy and figure designed and presented by the author using Datastream database and graphics.)

CORRECT PRICING OF ASIAN CRISIS IN AN EQUITY SPREAD

ASIA EX-JAPAN STOCK INDEX IN US$

CARREFOUR/PROMODES

FRENCH RETAILER PROMODES IS MOSTLY DOMESTIC ORIENTED

FRENCH RETAILER CARREFOUR HAS INTERNATIONAL EXPOSURE INCL. ASIA

Source: DATASTREAM

Figure 17.2

Correct pricing of the Asian crisis in a micro equity pair with a relative value component: Philips vs. Polygram (Dutch stocks). Philips, the Dutch consumer electronics group, owned 72 percent of Polygram in 1997—the Dutch music and film entertainment group (later in 1998 Philips sold its Polygram to Seagram). The Asian crisis primarily affected consumer electronics, PCs, and semiconductors, whereas entertainment was relatively less affected. While Philips was suffering in line with U.S. semiconductor stocks, investors defensively switched into Polygram, the more defensive component of Philips. The result is a stock ratio that perfectly tracks the Asian index.

(Original strategy and figure designed and presented by the author using Datastream database and graphics.)

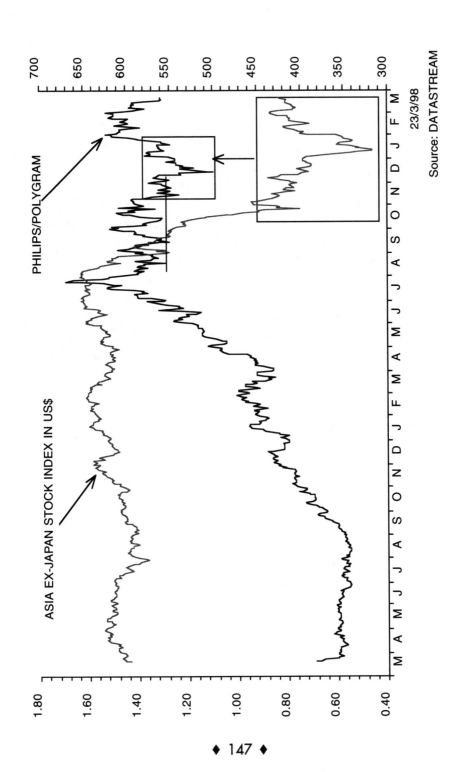

PHILIPS/POLYGRAM

ASIA EX-JAPAN STOCK INDEX IN US$

Source: DATASTREAM

23/3/98

Figure 17.3

The Asian crisis was correctly priced in the macro ratio between the relative performance of German and French car manufacturers sectors (local market exposure was hedged out with the spread between the German DAX and the French CAC40). Buying German car stocks hedged with short DAX futures and selling short French cars against long CAC 40 futures creates the relative return of German cars versus French cars when the local markets contributions are eliminated. Such a long/short macro position behaved identically to the Asia ex-Japan regional stock index in US $: this is because of the larger Asian exposure of German car exports.

The following sector indices were used:

French cars sector index	German cars sector index
Peugeot	Audi
Renault	BMW
	Daimler
	Ford
	Porsche
	Volkswagen

(Original strategy and figure designed and presented by the author using Datastream database and graphics.)

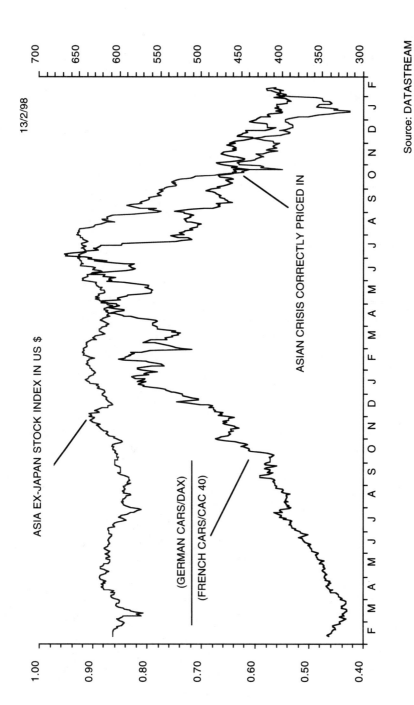

ASIA EX-JAPAN STOCK INDEX IN US $

(GERMAN CARS/DAX)
(FRENCH CARS/CAC 40)

ASIAN CRISIS CORRECTLY PRICED IN

13/2/98

Source: DATASTREAM

Mispricings of the Asian Crisis at the Top (Macro) Market Level (Sector and Stock Index Levels): Macroeconomic Arbitrage Opportunities

Markets quickly and correctly priced Asian crisis implications at the bottom market level involving relations (expressed by long/short equity spreads or switches) between individual stocks, such as in the Carrefour/Promodes and Philips/Polygram examples in Figures 17.1 and 17.2. As we move from the bottom up to higher integrated market levels, mispricings start appearing particularly at the top (macro) market level (i.e., at the level of relations between stock indices). The explanation is simple: the more information and relations about the implications of a macro event the market is trying to integrate at its top macro level, the higher the probability of misinterpretation and coding errors. This led to macroeconomic arbitrage opportunities in which, rather than having directional views (subjective macro trading strategies) on where Asian and global markets are going next, one is objectively measuring macroeconomic sensitivities of global markets to Asia and detecting mispriced representations of these sensitivities in long/short equity relations between two assets or two groups of assets. One advantage, among others, is to be able to play Asian effects not in a remote Asian market but in your own home markets (in the U.S. market, in European markets).

Figure 17.4 shows the relation between two of the European countries most exposed to Asia: Finland and Sweden. These markets are dominated by two telecommunications stocks, Nokia in Finland and Ericsson in Sweden, and the pulp and paper sector. Both telecommunications and paper sectors export heavily to Asia and make significant contributions to the GDP of the two countries. However, there is no major difference between the Asian exposures of the Finnish sector and the corresponding Swedish sector to explain why one market would be more affected than the other. Figure 17.4 shows that during the full-blown Asian crisis in the last squarter of 1997, the Finnish stock index (HEX) outperformed the Swedish stock index (OMX). The Finnish/Swedish equity market spread had a long history of tracking the performance of the Asia ex-Japan regional stock index except during the Asian crisis when the two diverged. Another exception to this tracking history is the second half of 1995 when Finland underperformed due to specific isolated problems with Nokia—which, like Ericsson, has a high weight in the respective stock market index—rather than due to any general market cause. One can actually measure the sensitivity betas of these and other markets with respect to the Asia ex-Japan regional stock index by using statistical regression analysis (see Table 17.1). If anything, Finland has a higher sensitivity beta than Sweden does, and it should have fallen by more than Sweden did.

We have thus collected the macroeconomic fundamental arguments (contribution to GDP of exports to Asia) and the quantitative arguments (sensitivity betas with respect to Asian stock markets) pointing to a macroeconomic mispricing of about 12 percent in the spread between Finnish and Swedish stock market indices, HEX/OMX. This mispricing was corrected over a few weeks, giving a 12 percent theoretical return on a spread that could have been implemented as a stock index futures spread. One possible reason for this macroeconomic mispricing is that while it is easier to assess the impact of a macro event on individual stocks, it is not so transparent to traders how much of

Table 17.1 Sensitivities (Betas) of Continental European Stock Indices with Respect to Asia Ex-Japan

Stock Index	Asian Sensitivity
Finland—HEX	0.513
Germany—DAX	0.480
Sweden—OMX	0.376
Netherlands—EOE	0.337
Spain—IBEX	0.300
Switzerland—SMI	0.300
Italy—MIB 30	0.267
France—CAC 40	0.264

Note: These betas represent the percentage change for 1 percent in the Asia ex-Japan regional stock index.

Figure 17.4

Mispricing of the Asian crisis in the macro ratio of equity markets Finland (HEX)/Sweden (OMX). Although the Asian exposures of Finland and Sweden are comparable, during the acute Asian crisis in the last quarter of 1997, the Swedish stock market overreacted by 12 percent, creating a macroeconomic arbitrage opportunity to sell Finnish stock index futures and to buy Swedish stock index futures for a 12 percent correction. Contributions to GDP by exports to Asia were similar in the two countries and so were the Asian exposures of the main two sectors of the two stock markets: pulp and paper and telecommunications.

(Original strategy and figure designed and presented by the author using Datastream database and graphics.)

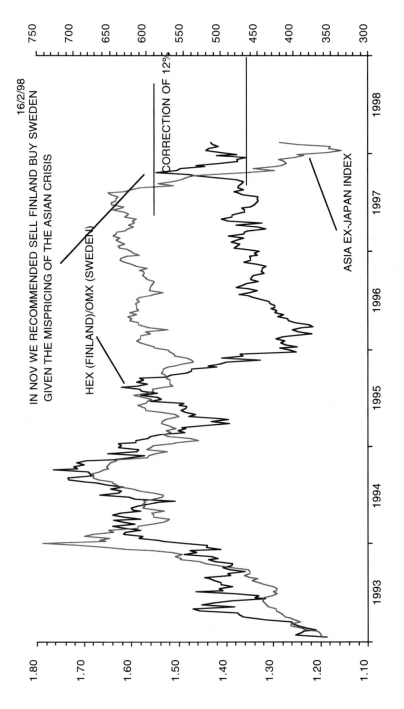

IN NOV WE RECOMMENDED SELL FINLAND BUY SWEDEN
GIVEN THE MISPRICING OF THE ASIAN CRISIS

16/2/98

CORRECTION OF 12%

HEX (FINLAND)/OMX (SWEDEN)

ASIA EX-JAPAN INDEX

Source: DATASTREAM

the total GDP is made by exports to Asia (macroeconomic impact) so that the impact on the whole market takes longer to be priced correctly. In this particular case it was probably more overreaction and panic in the more mature Swedish market when the crisis was finally fully acknowledged after a large overnight fall in Asian stock markets, given the known large exports to Asia of paper and telecommunications equipment and after the cancellation of large Asian projects (like the dam in Malaysia), which affected Swedish companies like ABB, a major name in the OMX index.

As proof of the importance of the pulp and paper sector, we get an almost identical macroeconomic mispricing in Figure 17.5. This suggested the macroeconomic arbitrage trade back in November 1997— long Swedish pulp and paper stocks/short Finnish pulp and paper stocks—for a 16 percent correction, which took place in a few weeks. Again, sensitivity betas of the two pulp and paper sectors suggest that the Finnish one should have been more affected than the Swedish one, so here is another agrument:

Sector	Asian sensitivity (beta)
Swedish pulp and paper sector	0.436
Finnish pulp and paper sector	0.603

Short-lived macroeconomic mispricings appeared at the sector level in the U.S. equity market. Although computer hardware stocks have much bigger Asian exposure (exports or sales to Asia) than do software stocks, during the Asian crisis hardware stocks outperformed the less exposed software stocks until the comments on the predicted slowdown in Asian demand for computers was acknowledged by the market and hardware stocks started underperforming. In this way, a macroeconomic mispricing gap of 5 percent was closed in 10 days (Figure 17.6). The efficiency and maturity of a market will always contribute to limiting the time scale of possible macroeconomic mispricings in markets of fast-developing global macro events like the Asian crisis. The trade in this case was short a basket of main Standard & Poor's

(S&P) 500 computer hardware stocks/long a basket of main S&P 500 software stocks (Figure 17.6).

Let us look next at one of those cross-equity market index spreads that had no visible relation with Asia until Asia became a problem and the market focused on a subliminal dormant relation between the Italian and the German stock markets based on German banks and companies having large loans and sales/projects in Asia relative to Italian banks and companies. The global macro event (Asian crisis) triggered this dormant relation, which was immediately activated (Italy outperformed Germany at the onset of the Asian crisis) as shown by Figure 17.7. However, a strong, four-year, upward, supporting trend of the German market outperforming the Italian one got in the way, and although Asia continued to fall, it took quite a while before Germany showed another episode of underperformance versus Italy. This was a clear macroeconomic arbitrage opportunity—sell German stock index futures (DAX)/buy Italian stock index futures (MIB 30)—starting from the moment the four-year, upward supporting trend was broken. This long-short macro spread was not chosen accidentally: there is a strong relation between Italy, entering in the first wave of the single-currency final stage of the European Monetary Union (EMU) in 1999, and Germany, "the anchor" of EMU. This was a second macro reason to expect the Italian equity market to finally start outperforming the German stock market because Italian short-term rates were expected to fall to converge with German rates (see Figures 3.2, 3.3, and 4.5).

Although French banks have a higher number of loans to Asia (potential "bad loans") relative to German banks, German banks like Deutsche Bank and Commerzbank addressed the issue early and in a transparent way by making much higher provisions for their exposure to Asia. Due to their good results, German banks remained in the black even after such large provisions. Despite this, the market decided that there was more corporate restructuring potential (mergers, takeovers) among French banks than among German banks. The restructuring stories in French banks go back at least to 1996, and by the end of 1997 we still did not see anything big. Meanwhile, in Germany,

Figure 17.5

Macroeconomic arbitrage of Asian crisis mispricing in the Finnish pulp and paper/Swedish pulp and paper sector price ratio. Although Finnish and Swedish pulp and paper stocks have comparable exposures in Asia, the Swedish pulp and paper sector overreacted to the Asian crisis, creating a macroeconomic arbitrage opportunity to sell a basket of Finnish pulp and paper and buy a basket of Swedish pulp and paper stocks.

The following sector indices were used:

Finnish pulp and paper sector index	Swedish pulp and paper sector index
Enso	Assidoman
Metsa Serla	Modo
UPM Kymmene	Stora
	SCA

(Original strategy and figure designed and presented by the author using Datastream database and graphics.)

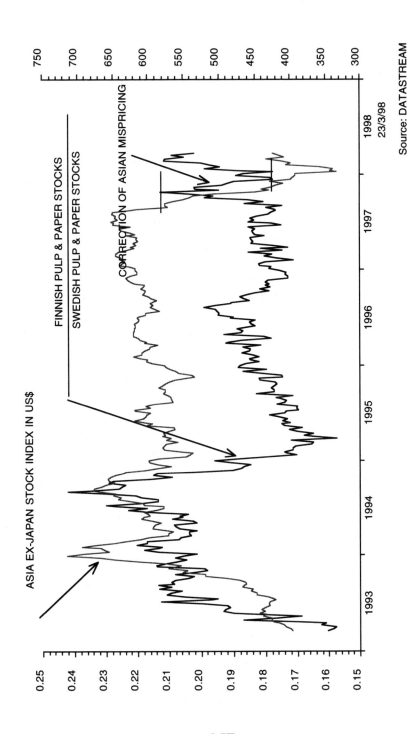

Figure 17.6

Short-term macro arbitrage based on the Asian crisis mispricing in the U.S. hardware stocks/software stocks ratio. The Asian exposure of U.S. hardware stocks is much bigger than the Asian exposure of U.S. software stocks. However, during the acute period of the Asian crisis in the last quarter of 1997, hardware stocks outperformed, thus creating a macro arbitrage opportunity to sell hardware stocks and buy software stocks for a 10 percent correction in 10 days.

The following sector indices were used:

U.S. S&P 500 software sector index	U.S. S&P 500 hardware sector index
Adobe Systems	Apple Computers
Autodesk	Compaq Computers
Computer Associates	Data General
Computer Sciences	DELL Computers
HBO	Digital Equipment
Microsoft	Hewlett-Packard
Novell	IBM
Oracle Corporation	Silicon Graphics
Parametric Tech.	Sun Microsystems
Unisys	

(Original strategy and figure designed and presented by the author using Datastream database and graphics.)

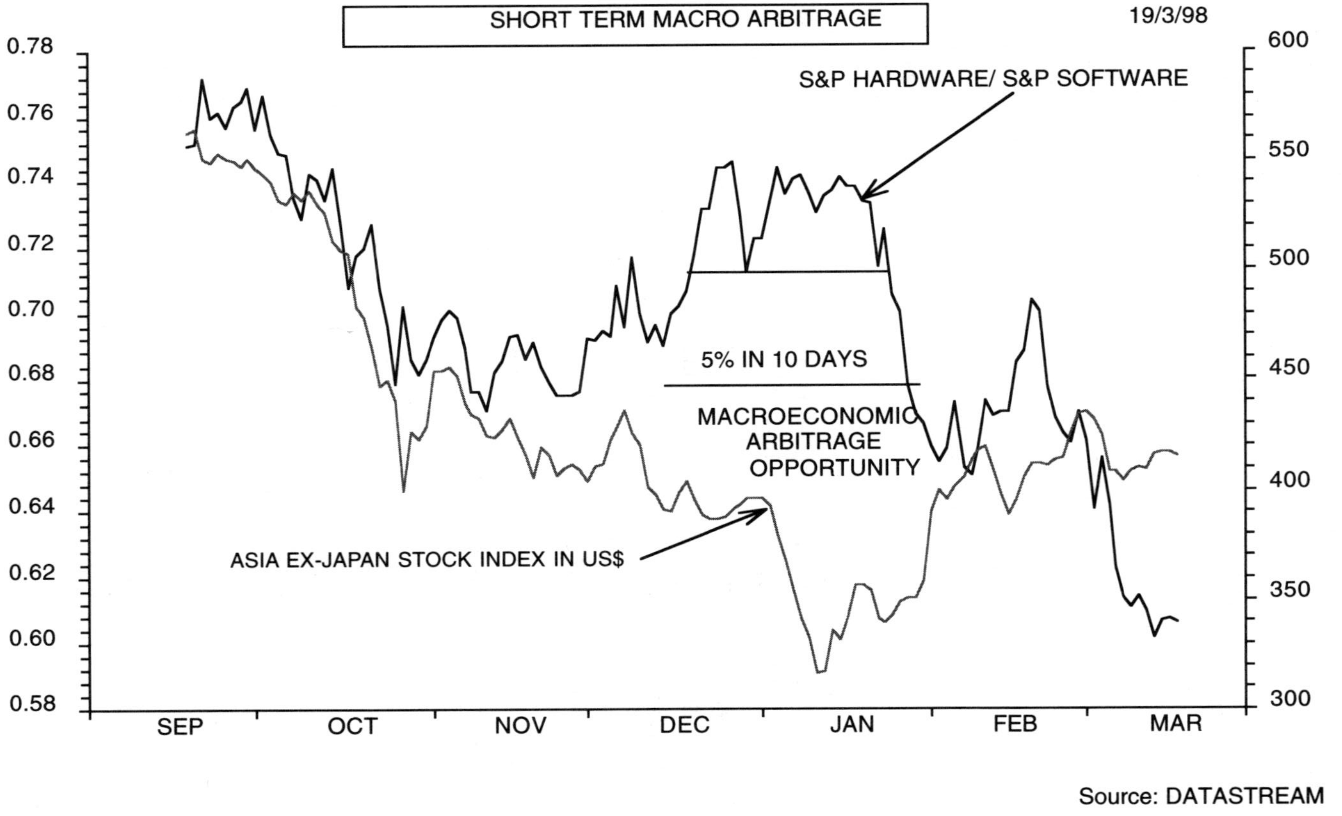

SHORT TERM MACRO ARBITRAGE
19/3/98
S&P HARDWARE/ S&P SOFTWARE
5% IN 10 DAYS
MACROECONOMIC
ARBITRAGE
OPPORTUNITY
ASIA EX-JAPAN STOCK INDEX IN US$
0.78
0.76
0.74
0.72
0.70
0.68
0.66
0.64
0.62
0.60
0.58
600
550
500
450
400
350
300
SEP
OCT
NOV
DEC
JAN
FEB
MAR
Source: DATASTREAM

Figure 17.7

Asian crisis mispricing in the Germany/Italy stock market spread (DAX/COMIT 30). German banks' exposure to Asia via bad loans is much bigger than any similar exposure of Italian banks. However the temperamental Italian market overreacted to the fall of the Asian markets, creating a macro arbitrage opportunity to buy Italy and sell Germany. A significant historic support trendline can also be blamed for the delayed correct pricing of Asia in this stock market ratio.

(Original strategy and figure designed and presented by the author using Datastream database and graphics.)

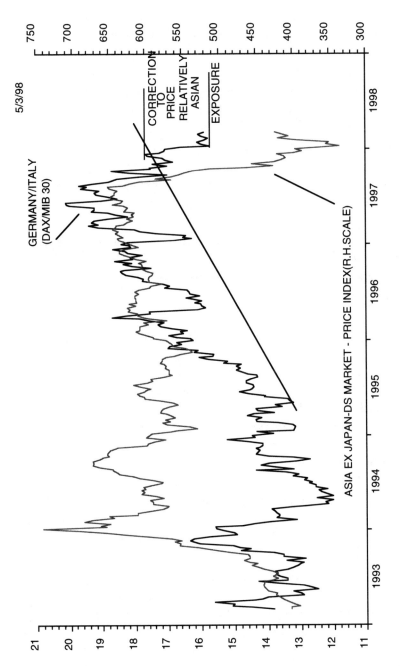

5/3/98

750
700
650
600
550
500
450
400
350
300

CORRECTION
TO
PRICE
RELATIVELY
ASIAN
EXPOSURE

GERMANY/ITALY
(DAX/MIB 30)

ASIA EX JAPAN-DS MARKET - PRICE INDEX(R.H.SCALE)

1993 1994 1995 1996 1997 1998

21
20
19
18
17
16
15
14
13
12
11

Source: DATASTREAM

Bayerische Hypo merged with Bayerische Vereinsbank. As a result of these market expectations, French banks had a better relative performance (relative to local market stock index CAC 40) than that of German banks (relative to local market stock index DAX) during the beginnings of the Asian crisis in the fall of 1997. A clear mispricing gap was open in Figure 17.8, which finally started to respond correctly to the Asian-yen-weakness-driven relapse of Asia from the middle of 1998. There is still as much as 20 percent correction potential if no major mergers refocus markets on French banks. One explanation might be the interim reporting system of German banks that French banks do not have. It will take much longer before markets can have an idea of the impact of Asia on French banks, and it might be then that German banks start outperforming. Again, as in the case of French car stocks/German car stocks, we eliminated the local market contribution (market factor) to the spread between the two banking sectors by following the ratio

(French banks/stock index CAC 40)/
(German banks/stock index DAX)

The macroeconomic arbitrage of the mispricing of Asian exposures in the spread between the relative performance of French banks and the relative performance of German banks with respect to their corresponding local stock market indices can be implemented as the following long/short macro positions:

long German banks, short DAX futures

short French banks, long CAC 40 futures

This is a rare case where the macro event could not get the market focused on the relation between French and German banks vis-a-vis their exposures to Asia. This subliminal (dormant) relation has yet perhaps to be fully activated. Justified or not, this happened because of fears of long-term restructuring in the French banking sector that might cover temporary bad results due to bad Asian loans.

The General Model of Macro-Event-Triggered Subliminal (Dormant) Macro Relations in Global Markets

We conclude this chapter by formalizing the general model of how a macro event (the Asian crisis, in this case) reactivates and brings into the spotlight dormant, subliminal relations between assets in global markets. Existing relations that did not matter suddenly become visible.

Recall the Carrefour and Promodes example earlier in this chapter. Under normal market conditions Asian stock market moves do not lead to moves in the ratio Carrefour/Promodes. However as soon as a macro event in Asia triggered a sharp move in Asian stock markets exceeding a certain very high threshold, Asia mattered and the balance between Carrefour and Promodes changed.

Figure 17.9 contains the symbolic general representation of our model using some specific price historic series. The Asian crisis is the *macro event* and the Asia ex-Japan regional stock index is the *macro event representative asset*. Philips relative to the Dutch stock index and Philadelphia semiconductor stock index relative to the S&P 500 are two spreads of assets or relative performances of two assets that under normal market circumstances have no visible correlation with the Asia ex-Japan regional stock index, although here are two dormant, inactive, subliminal macro relations: U.S. semiconductor stocks and Philips export or sell heavily in the fast-growing Asian markets. So there are existing subliminal relations between these assets and the macro event representative asset. However these correlations are not observable in Figure 17.9 until Asia stops growing and goes into crisis and perhaps into recession (the macro event) as it happened dramatically in October 1997. Then suddenly, the Asia ex-Japan regional index and the relative performances of Philips and U.S. semiconductor stocks started moving together (subliminal relations are triggered by the macro event, and the price moves of the two assets become strongly connected to the macro event representative asset). When the intensity of the macro event decreases significantly so that market does not focus on it like before, the two assets or even just one of them diverge from the macro

Figure 17.8

Macroeconomic mispricing of Asian crisis in the French banks/German banks ratio with currency adjustment and local markets hedged out (hedged with CAC 40/DAX spread). French banks, such as Societe Generale and Credit Lyonnais, have a considerably higher exposure to Asia through bad loans than do German banks, such as Deutsche Bank, Dresdner, and Commerzbank. Moreover, a better performance allowed German banks to make more significant provisions earlier in expectation of future losses and to still report interim figures in the black. Altogether, excluding the contribution of the local market factor, French banks should have outperformed German banks. However, a higher expectation of restructuring and speculations led to the opposite mispriced reaction. This is a macroeconomic arbitrage opportunity to sell French banks, buy German banks and to hedge exposure to local markets in France and Germany by selling DAX/CAC 40 spread.

The following sector indices were used:

French banks sector index	German banks sector index
Bancaire	Bayerische Hypo
BNP	Bayerische Vereinsbank
CCF	BHF
Credit Lyonnais	Commerzbank
Natexis	Deutsche
Dexia	Dresdner
Paribas	
Societe Generale	
and others	and others

(Original strategy and figure designed and presented by the author using Datastream database and graphics.)

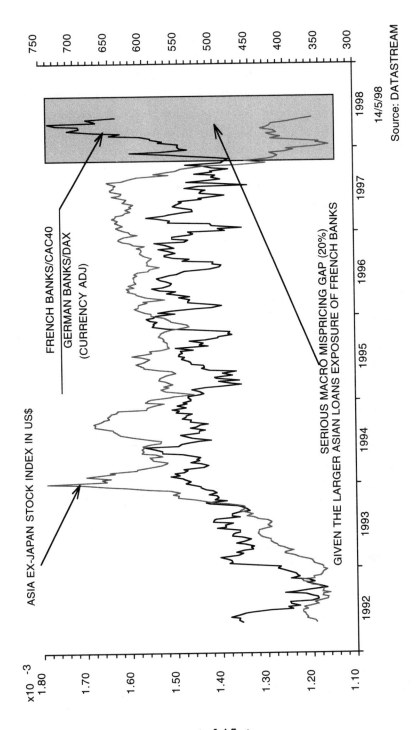

ASIA EX-JAPAN STOCK INDEX IN US$

FRENCH BANKS/CAC40
GERMAN BANKS/DAX
(CURRENCY ADJ)

SERIOUS MACRO MISPRICING GAP (20%)
GIVEN THE LARGER ASIAN LOANS EXPOSURE OF FRENCH BANKS

14/5/98

Source: DATASTREAM

Figure 17.9

The symbolic general model ot *macro event* (Asian crisis) triggered and synchronized *subliminal (dormant) macro relations in global markets* (the relation between semiconductors and consumer electronics stocks on one side and Asian stock markets on the other side). The relation between Philips/Polygram and the Asian crisis discussed in Figure 17.2 is only a slice of a bigger pie! Semiconductor stocks in the United States (here we used the Philadelphia semiconductor index) have underperformed the S&P 500 in the same way as Philips, relative to the Dutch index EOE, did in the Netherlands during the Asian crisis: these two examples are global slices of a much more general macro relation, one between consumer electronics and the macroeconomics of Asia. The U.S. market was much faster to price in this subliminal dormant macro relation because semiconductor stocks started underperforming in August 1997 due to the Asian fall, whereas in the Dutch market, Philips only started underperforming the Dutch index in October, after the second attack of Asian ills. At that time, both U.S. semiconductors and Philips performances relative to the two local markets started behaving synchronously after delayed triggering by the common macro event (the Asian crisis). There was no similarity, no coupling, among the behaviors of the Asia ex-Japan regional index, Philips relative to EOE, and the Philadelphia semiconductor stock index relative to the S&P 500 prior to October 1997 when the three converged. After May 1998 they diverged (decoupling), given the fading of Asian fears that had brought them together in the first place.

General model: Several noncorrelated spreads of assets converge and become correlated (coupled) after a macro event (represented by some macro asset price move) activates (triggers) the subliminal (dormant) relations between these spreads of assets and the dynamics of the macro event representative asset (the market remembers forgotten or once irrelevant relations and focuses on them). As soon as the market shifts its focus from the macro event and its representative asset, the spreads of assets decouple from each other and from the macro event representative asset, and they all diverge.

(Original strategy and figure designed and presented by the author using Datastream database and graphics.)

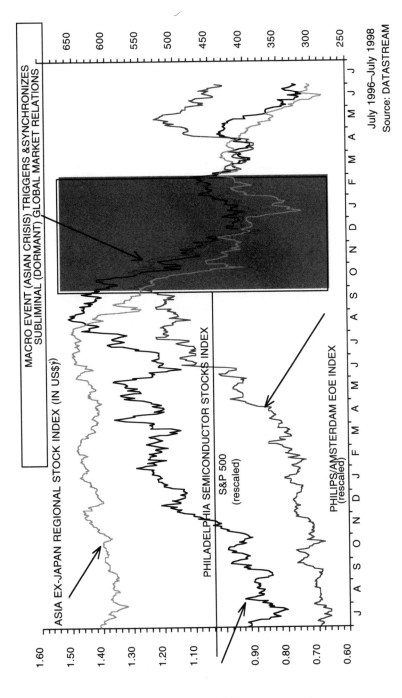

MACRO EVENT (ASIAN CRISIS) TRIGGERS &SYNCHRONIZES
SUBLIMINAL (DORMANT) GLOBAL MARKET RELATIONS

ASIA EX-JAPAN REGIONAL STOCK INDEX (IN US$)

PHILADELPHIA SEMICONDUCTOR STOCKS INDEX

S&P 500
(rescaled)

PHILIPS/AMSTERDAM EOE INDEX
(rescaled)

July 1996–July 1998
Source: DATASTREAM

event representative asset. It's over; it does not matter anymore. The macro relations are inactivated, put to sleep, and return to their dormant subliminal state until the next onset of this macro event or of any related macro event.

Chapter **18**

Macro Arbitrage of EMU Convergence Mispricings in Equity Markets

In 1999, a single European currency, the *Euro*, will be introduced in 11 European countries as part of the final stage of achieving the European Monetary Union (EMU). The 11 countries are: Austria, Belgium, Finland, France, Germany, Ireland, Italy, Luxembourg, the Netherlands, Portugal, and Spain. As was already pointed out in Chapters 3 and 4, this implied a convergence process ahead of 1999 (we called it *Euroconvergence*) of the short-term interest rates of EMU countries to the short-term rates of Germany, "the anchor of the EMU." In Chapters 3 and 4, we saw how to take advantage of these falling interest rates macroeconomic views in directional and long/short macro strategies, respectively.

It is time now to switch from subjective macroeconomic views on the EMU to objective macroeconomic mispricings of the Euroconvergence process in equity markets. As we do not use our views, we need an approach to read objectively what is priced in the markets about the future of short-term interest rates. Suppose it is November 1997, and we want to know what is priced in the markets concerning the future of interest rates in Italy and Spain, two strong EMU candidates that have already come down a long way from their "high yielders" interest rates toward German rates. What about the near future in three months' or six months' time? The answer is in the interest rate futures markets of Italy and Spain: Eurolira futures and Europeseta futures. "One hundred minus the price of these interest rate futures" is the expected future value of three months' interest rates. We just want to objectively check what is priced in markets concerning the future rate cuts in Italy and Spain that are needed to achieve convergence to German rates. Figures 18.1 and 18.2 show the way to read the mind of the market concerning the future expected difference between rate cuts to come in Italy and rate cuts to come in Spain back in November 1997:

Italian expected rate cuts (3 months) =
Eurolira March 1998 – Eurolira December 1997

Spanish expected rate cuts (3 months) =
Europeseta March 1998 – Europeseta December 1997

These give the difference between the two evaluated at around 50 basis points (bps), or 0.5 percent, more rate cuts to come in Italy than in Spain. How about the future of rate cuts differential up to June 1998 (six months)? We get similarly:

Italian expected rate cuts (6 months) =
Eurolira June 1998 – Eurolira December 1997

Spanish expected rate cuts (6 months) =
Europeseta June 1998 – Europeseta December 1997

giving an indication of 80 basis points (bps), or 0.8 percent, more rate cuts to come in Italy. Of course, all these are approximate indications, and they refer to three months' rates rather than the real short-term rates. The element of uncertainty is quite important because several times in 1997 and 1998, political crises in Italy that related to their long-term budget plan as well as to their economic statistics revelations (like the GDP—gross domestic product) raised a question mark about Italy's presence in the first wave of the EMU that it might not satisfy the EMU joining criterion relating debt to GDP.

Having established what is priced in markets about the difference between future rate cuts in Italy versus future rate cuts in Spain, we have in our hands a *macroeconomic EMU relative convergence indicator*, or *variable*, for Italian versus Spanish rates (*future expected interest rate*

Figure 18.1

Reading the difference between the expectations of interest rate futures markets in Spain and Italy in November 1997. Due to their 1999 entry in the final single currency phase of the EMU, Italian (Eurolira) and Spanish (Europeseta) futures markets priced in November 1997 50 bps more rate cuts to come in Italy than in Spain over the following three months.

(Original figure designed and presented by the author using Datastream database and graphics.)

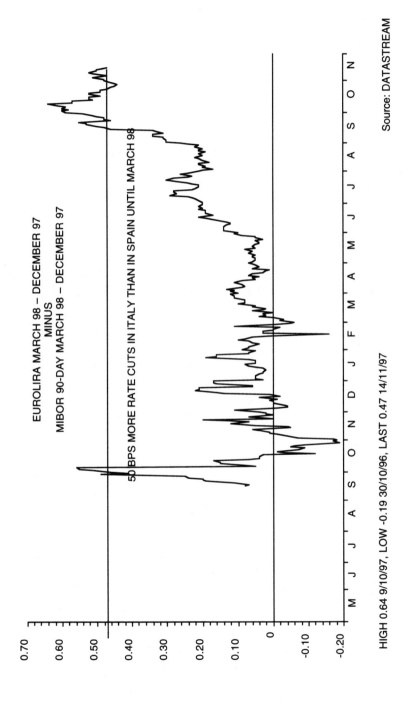

EUROLIRA MARCH 98 – DECEMBER 97
MINUS
MIBOR 90-DAY MARCH 98 – DECEMBER 97

50 BPS MORE RATE CUTS IN ITALY THAN IN SPAIN UNTIL MARCH 98

HIGH 0.64 9/10/97, LOW -0.19 30/10/96, LAST 0.47 14/11/97

Source: DATASTREAM

Figure 18.2

Reading the difference between the expectations of interest rate futures markets in Spain and Italy in November 1997. Due to their 1999 entry in the final single currency phase of the EMU, Italian (Eurolira) and Spanish (Europeseta) futures markets priced in November 1997 80 bps more rate cuts to come in Italy than in Spain over the following six months.

(Original figure designed and presented by the author using Datastream database and graphics.)

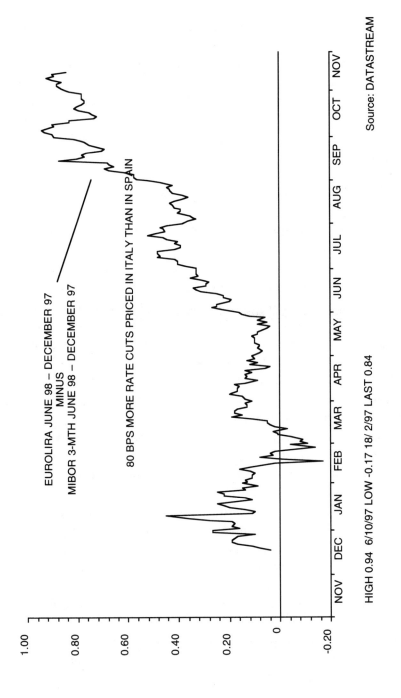

EUROLIRA JUNE 98 – DECEMBER 97
MINUS
MIBOR 3-MTH JUNE 98 – DECEMBER 97

80 BPS MORE RATE CUTS PRICED IN ITALY THAN IN SPAIN

HIGH 0.94 6/10/97 LOW -0.17 18/ 2/97 LAST 0.84

Source: DATASTREAM

cuts differential), and we can start checking whether equity markets are pricing this convergence differential accordingly at all times. This is one of the special cases we hinted at when we presented the general macroeconomic arbitrage model in Chapter 5: the macro variable is not some economic statistic but because it is a function of interest rates, it can be represented as a spread of traded instruments (futures), in fact, a spread between two calendar spreads of interest rate futures. In Figure 18.3, we can see how the ratio between the relative performance of Italian banks (relative to local stock index MIB 30) and the relative performance of Spanish banks (relative to local stock index IBEX) is pricing in the difference between the rate cuts to come in Italy and the rate cuts to come in Spain (future/expected-interest-rate-cuts differential) as we move in time.

The equity spread and the interest-rate-expectations differential should track each other because banks are interest-rate-sensitive stocks; and if there are more rate cuts to come in Italy, then Italian banks should outperform their local market and, indeed, should outperform the Spanish banks (relative to their local markets). If, however, bad things happened and it did not look as though Italy would be in the EMU in 1999, then whichever way the interest-rate-cut-expectation differential pointed, the balance between the relative performances of Italian and Spanish banks should lean the same way.

A serious macroeconomic mispricing appeared in February 1998: Italian banks underperformed Spanish banks relative to their local markets, despite the future expected-rate-cut differential between Italy and Spain continuing to point in favor of Italy. Given the fact that here the macro variable can be directly represented by traded instruments, rather than doing a macroeconomic arbitrage trade based solely on the upward correction in Italian banks/Spanish banks relative performance ratio, we can add the other "leg" of the macroeconomic arbitrage saying that both the asset spread and the macroeconomic variables spread have to reconverge to each other. So the future expected-interest-rate-cuts differential in this particular case must correct slightly downward (see Figure 18.3). The full long market asset ratio/short macroeconomic ratio trade can be implemented thus by the following positions:

Macro Arbitrage: EMU Convergence

Long equity position: Italian banks, IBEX futures
Long interest rate futures : June 1998 Eurolira, September 1998
Europeseta

versus

Short equity position: Spanish banks, MIB 30 futures
Short interest rate futures: September 1998 Eurolira, June 1998
Europeseta with FX lira/peseta hedge

As a version of this macroeconomic arbitrage strategy, we can consider the ratio between the absolute performance of Italian banks and of Spanish banks without factoring out the two local markets. This cross-market equity-sector spread depends not only on the Italian/Spanish interest rate differential but also on the performance of the Italian stock market as a whole, relative to the Spanish stock market, MIB 30/IBEX. One can then assume that ahead of the 1999 EMU, MIB 30/IBEX itself is dependent on the Italian/Spanish interest rate differential only. Figure 18.4 shows three macroeconomic mispricings and the way they corrected. The January 1998 mispricing had a higher probability of success as a macroeconomic arbitrage opportunity than did the September 1997 and October 1997 ones. The reason for this is related to the role of other secondary macroeconomic variables in a given macroeconomic arbitrage trade. The GDP growth in Italy caught up with the Spanish GDP growth only at the end of 1998. Because one could still hear at that time the argument in favor of higher corporate earnings in Spain (see Figure 4.6), September 1997 and perhaps October 1997 were too early to be long Italy/short Spain. Also the expectation and reality of corporate restructurings in the banking sector had one favorite only—Italy. Therefore, do not short Italian banks. The January 1998 macroeconomic arbitrage strategy gets right the interest rate differential and recommends buying the Italian banks that were effervescently restructuring at that time with an Italian GDP in full steam (at least according to recent past statistics).

Figure 18.3

Macroeconomic arbitrage based on EMU Convergence mispricing in the Italian banks/Spanish banks relative market performance spread. As interest-rate-sensitive stocks, banks in Italy and Spain should track the corresponding interest rate expectations in the two interest rate futures markets. In February 1998, a mispricing gap appears between the Italian banks relative to market/Spanish banks relative to market ratio and the differential of rate-cut expectations in the two countries given the need to converge to German rates ahead of the 1999 EMU. This was a clear macroeconomic arbitrage opportunity to sell Spanish banks and buy Spanish stock index (IBEX) futures while buying Italian banks and selling Italian stock index (MIB 30) futures. This is one of the macro arbitrages where the macro variables are directly expressed by a spread of interest rate futures: September1998 Eurolira contract – June1998 Eurolira + June1998 Europeseta – September1998 Europeseta. To take full advantage of the mispricing gap created in February1998, we can buy the bottom equity ratio (spread) and sell the top macroeconomic ratio expressed as interest rate futures spread. In its most complete expression this macro arbitrage trade takes the form:

Long equity position: Italian banks, IBEX futures
Long interest rate futures: June1998 Eurolira, September 1998 Europeseta

versus

Short equity position: Spanish banks, MIB 30 futures
Short interest rate futures: September1998 Eurolira, June1998 Europeseta with FX Lira/Peseta hedge

The following sector indices were used:

Italian banks sector index	Spanish banks sector index
Banca di Roma	Argentaria
Fideuram	BBV
Banca Intesa	BCH
COMIT	Popular
Credito Italiano	Santander
IMI	Banesto
San Paolo Torino	Bankinter
and others	and others

(Original strategy and figure designed and presented by the author using Datastream database and graphics.)

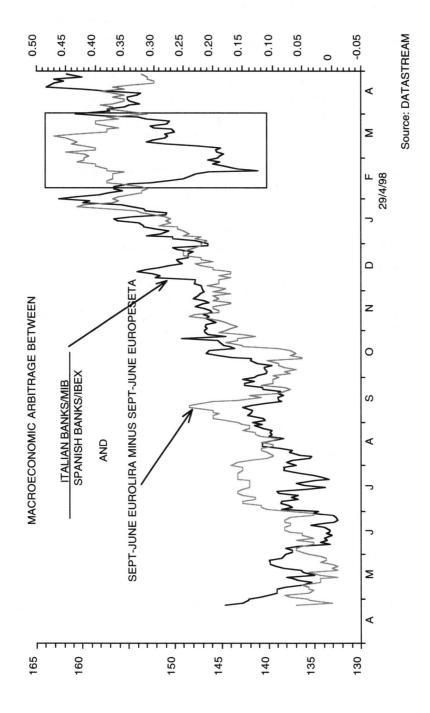

MACROECONOMIC ARBITRAGE BETWEEN

ITALIAN BANKS/MIB
SPANISH BANKS/IBEX

AND

SEPT-JUNE EUROLIRA MINUS SEPT-JUNE EUROPESETA

29/4/98

Source: DATASTREAM

Figure 18.4

Macroeconomic arbitrage of interest-rate expectations mispricings in Italian banks/Spanish banks absolute performance ratio. As opposed to Figure 18.3, we consider here the absolute performance ratio between Italian and Spanish banks without hedging out the local market exposures. We can see three highlighted macro mispricings of the expected-interest-rate-cuts differential in the sector absolute performance ratio Italian banks/Spanish banks. These macro arbitrage opportunities are different from the one in Figure 18.3 where the sector-relative-to-market performance ratio was considered. In a way, we consider here mispricings of interest-rate expectations in both the banking stocks sector and the local stock market. Usually, the macroeconomic variables spread is not expressed in terms of tradable instruments. As in Figure 18.3 we can use interest rate futures to trade the equity spread against the macroeconomic variables spread. The mispricing of January1998 created the macro arbitrage opportunity:

Long Italian banks/Short Spanish banks with FX peseta/lira hedge

or in its most complete form (sell macro variables spread, buy equity spread):

Long equity position: Italian banks
Long interest rate futures: June1998 Eurolira,
September1998 Europeseta

versus

Short equity position: Spanish banks
Short interest rate futures: September1998 Eurolira,
June1998 Europeseta with FX Peseta/Lira hedge

The following sector indices were used:

Italian banks sector index	Spanish banks sector index
Banca di Roma	Argentaria
Fideuram	BBV
Banca Intesa	BCH
COMIT	Popular
Credito Italiano	Santander
IMI	Banesto
San Paolo Torino	Bankinter
and others	and others

(Original strategy and figure designed and presented by the author using Datastream database and graphics.)

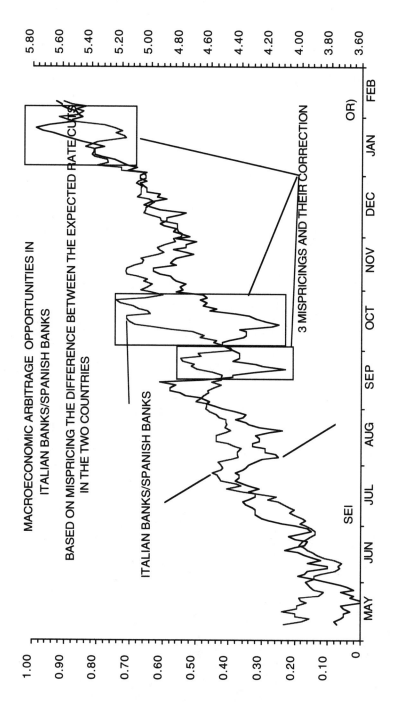

MACROECONOMIC ARBITRAGE OPPORTUNITIES IN
ITALIAN BANKS/SPANISH BANKS

BASED ON MISPRICING THE DIFFERENCE BETWEEN THE EXPECTED RATE CUTS
IN THE TWO COUNTRIES

ITALIAN BANKS/SPANISH BANKS

3 MISPRICINGS AND THEIR CORRECTION

Source: DATASTREAM

♦ 181 ♦

Chapter 19

Macro Mispricings of Currencies (Exchange Rates) in Stock Markets

Together with interest rates, exchange rates are one of the most important macroeconomic control variables. It is no wonder that the most famous macro trades of all times are currency trades (part of the reason for this is the great liquidity of foreign exchange [FX] markets). Exchange rates influence the performance of companies by shaping the domestic value of earnings on exports and on nondomestic activities. As a consequence, stock markets are extremely sensitive to currency moves. The French stock market is one of the most dollar-sensitive stock markets in Europe; that is, stock index CAC 40 depends on French franc/US dollar exchange rates. Often, given the higher volatility of stock markets, equities amplify currency moves.

Let us look at an example based on the big dollar rally of 1997, which was one of the main engines of the 1997 bull market. The dollar is priced in equity markets according to the dollar sensitivity of stock returns, and one can measure the beta-sensitivity of a stock with respect to the dollar by regressing stock returns on exchange rate returns. This statistically derived measure—call this beta "currency beta" or "dollar beta" to distinguish it from the market beta—indicates the percentage that the stock return increases for a 1 percent rally (strengthening) in the exchange rate (in this case French franc/US dollar). The dollar beta is a measure similar to the market beta of a stock with respect to the stock market index, for which one uses statistical regression of stock returns versus stock market index returns. Figure 19.1

shows a basket of the 12 highest dollar-sensitive stocks in the French stock index CAC 40. The dollar betas were measured at the end of 1996 using one-year price information. It was at that stage that French senior politicians pointed to the benefits for the French economy to have a weaker French franc or, equivalently, a strong dollar. The end of 1996 and the beginning of 1997 saw many famous traders betting on a strong dollar rally. The rally did indeed come, as one can see in Figure 19.1, and our basket of dollar-sensitive stocks rallied even more. Starting from the first day in January 1997 until mid-February, the dollar rallied 9.6 percent, and our dollar-sensitive basket proved indeed hypersensitive by rallying 16 percent. Figure 19.1 shows how closely stock markets track currencies and how accurately the dollar is priced in European stock markets. Of course, whereas a European company benefits from a dollar rally by increasing the value in domestic currency of foreign earnings, this is not the case for U.S. companies because foreign earnings will translate to fewer and fewer dollars if the dollar strengthens.

We have learned so far that it is very likely for European stocks of companies that export a lot or that have subsidiaries abroad to have a higher dollar sensitivity. Very often these exporters or internationally spread companies are among the blue-chip stocks—stocks with the highest market capitalization—because the size of their internationally diversified businesses is larger than the average domestically oriented companies. That is why in Europe the ratio blue chips/total market or, in particular, blue chips/mid-caps (stocks with average market capitalization) reflects the US dollar. In Figure 19.2 we used the new cross-market pan-EMU (European Monetary Union) Euroland or Eurozone indices Dow Jones EURO STOXX, which will be discussed in Chapter 20. These indices include stocks selected (using market capitalization and liquidity) from the main stock indices of the 11 countries that will join the first wave of EMU's final stage in 1999 when a single European currency will be introduced. Rather than being focused on one European market, we wanted a pan-European example, so we took the top 50 Euroland blue chips and the broad Euromarket index (330 stocks) to get a ratio of the Euro blue chips index to the Euromarket index: Dow Jones Euro STOXX 50/Dow Jones EURO

Figure 19.1

A basket of dollar-sensitive French stocks tracks and in fact outperforms the French franc/US dollar exchange rate. Currency exchange rate is priced in the market according to the dollar sensitivity (dollar beta) of the stocks. From January 1, 1997, to Mid-February 1997, a basket of equally weighted, French, dollar-sensitive stocks (an alternative is dollar sensitivity weighted to enhance the currency effect) has rallied 16 percent compared to the dollar, which strengthened (French franc weakened) by 9.6 percent (beta sensitivity of 1.66).

The following stocks have been selected in the basket based on historic dollar sensitivity analysis using statistic regression:

Schneider	Sanofi	Elf
Renault	Legrand	Total
Lafarge	Pernod-Ricard	LVMH
L'Oreal	Carrefour	St. Gobain

(Original strategy and figure designed and presented by the author using Datastream database and graphics.)

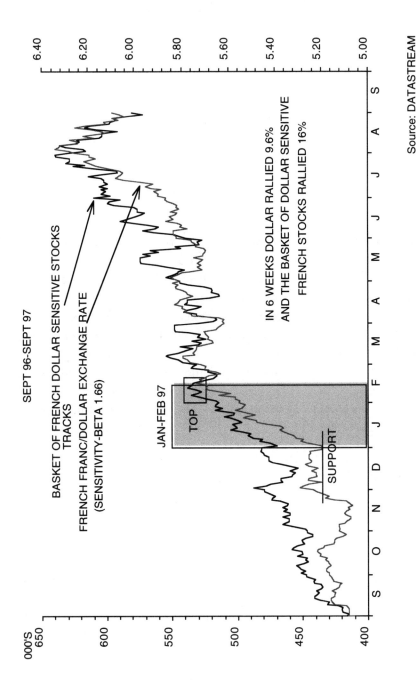

SEPT 96-SEPT 97

BASKET OF FRENCH DOLLAR SENSITIVE STOCKS
TRACKS

FRENCH FRANC/DOLLAR EXCHANGE RATE
(SENSITIVITY-BETA 1.66)

IN 6 WEEKS DOLLAR RALLIED 9.6%
AND THE BASKET OF DOLLAR SENSITIVE
FRENCH STOCKS RALLIED 16%

JAN-FEB 97

TOP

SUPPORT

Source: DATASTREAM

Figure 19.2

Macro mispricings of exchange rates in the EMU (Eurozone) blue chips relative performance ratio: pan-European macroeconomic arbitrage. The performance of the top-50 Eurozone blue chips index (Dow Jones Euro STOXX 50) relative to the broad index Dow Jones Euro STOXX (representing the new 11-market pan-EMU Eurozone) is dependent on the ECU/US $ exchange rates: if the dollar strengthens, blue chips (which are heavy exporters) outperform mid-caps (more domestically oriented). A macroeconomic mispricing appeared at the beginning of 1998 as Asian fears caused the exporters to underperform. If the dollar remains at this level, we should soon see a correction in favor of Euro blue chips.

(Original strategy and figure designed and presented by the author using Datastream database and graphics.)

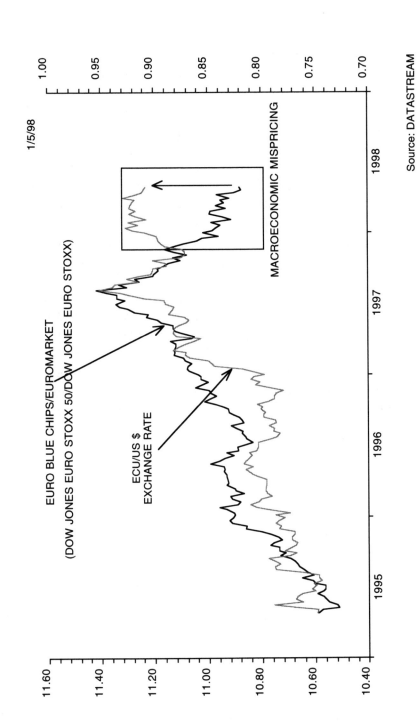

1/5/98

EURO BLUE CHIPS/EUROMARKET
(DOW JONES EURO STOXX 50/DOW JONES EURO STOXX)

ECU/US $
EXCHANGE RATE

MACROECONOMIC MISPRICING

Source: DATASTREAM

STOXX. Before the introduction in 1999 of the single European currency, the Euro, we can still use ECU (European currency unit) as a basket of European currencies that has been in place for several years. As expected, the ECU/US $ exchange rate is correctly priced in the ratio Euro blue chips/Euromarket. The two track each other reasonably well up to the end of 1997 when although the dollar continued strengthening, blue chips started seriously underperforming the market in the EMU Euromarket. It is a mispricing that in the future should be corrected, but there is an explanation for this wide gap: the Asian crisis. Even if exports are bringing dollar revenues, if the total volume of exports is falling, then the total dollar revenues are falling—and that is exactly the expectation that got priced in the market at the end of 1997. However as we went through 1998, we repeatedly saw companies and economists pointing to the exaggerated Asian worries and stating the limited Asian impact. Exports to Asia are a limited fraction of total exports of European corporations, and strong dollar revenues from the other exports should help compensate for the Asian crisis effect. If the dollar does not weaken significantly, the gap opened at the end of 1996 between the dollar and the relative performance of Euro blue chips should narrow and close.

Chapter 20

Long/Short Macro Spreads and Macro Arbitrage Opportunities within the New EMU Euro Stock Markets

Macro Arbitrage in Euroland

European markets structure will be reshaped in 1999 by the introduction of a single European currency, the Euro. This is part of the final stage of the process of achieving the European Monetary Union (EMU). A politically and financially integrated, or at least coordinated, Europe will gradually lead to the creation of a new pan-European, Eurozone, or Euroland integrated stock market involving the stock markets of the 11 countries to join in 1999 in the first wave of the EMU: Austria, Belgium, Finland, France, Germany, Ireland, Italy, Luxembourg, the Netherlands, Portugal, and Spain. This is an unusual macro experience—or should I say a "macro experiment" —because one will have the chance to see in time the birth of a new "macro playground": the monetary and politically integrated Euroland market. It is comparable *metaphorically* to the chance (which history did not give us) to see the U.S. stock market being born out of 50 states' stock markets. Of course, this assumes that everything will be okay and that the final stage of the EMU will be successfully completed, leading to further pan-European integration. This process will take time, which means that initially there will be a lot of pan-European Eurozone *macro inefficiencies* that can be speculated by long/short macro and macroeconomic arbitrage trading and investment strategies in the first few years after January 1, 1999.

We need first of all a general integrative model for the overall stock market of the 11 countries' Eurozone. Our general model should differentiate between inside-Eurozone and outside-Eurozone, between top EMU blue chips and the overall Euro stock market. One such general framework is provided by the Dow Jones STOXX family of stock indices and sector indices that was introduced ahead of the 1999 final stage of the EMU (Figure 20.1). It contains a 330-stock Dow Jones Euro STOXX index and a top-50-blue-chips Dow Jones Euro STOXX 50 index. The stocks were selected from the main stock indices of the 11 countries on the basis of market capitalization and liquidity, with some maximum-limit weight restrictions per sector per country in order to ensure a wide representation of the 11 individual stock markets. In order to characterize with a consistent index the general European stock market environment, including both EMU and non-EMU, the 660-stock Dow Jones STOXX index was introduced together with the corresponding top-50-blue-chip Dow Jones STOXX 50 index. These are not just theoretical indices. Some have listed futures already trading, such as Dow Jones Euro STOXX 50 futures and Dow Jones STOXX 50 futures. The launching and listing of these Euro stock index futures was done in coordination with the main continental European exchanges.

The single European currency, the Euro, and the short-term rates converging to the German anchor short rates are a strong starting basis for a Euro (EMU) macroeconomics. Therefore, it makes a lot of sense to explore the country weight and the sector weight structures of the new Euro stock indices. One of the best ways to characterize a new entity is by comparison with the environment from which it emerged. Table 20.1 shows the differences in country weighting and sector weighting between Euro STOXX 50 and STOXX 50 based on April 1998 data provided by Deutsche Bourse.

The first observation is that in terms of country weights, the Eurozone stock universe is, of course, dominated by France, Germany, and (surprise) the Netherlands (Holland). The big absentees are the

DOW JONES STOXX INDEX

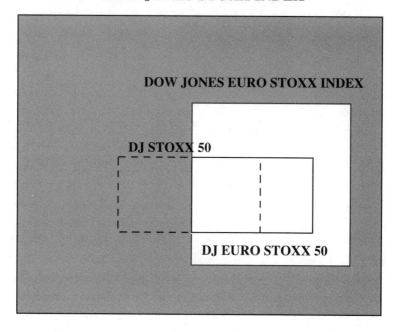

RELATIONS BETWEEN THE STOCK UNIVERSES OF
DOW JONES STOXX INDICES

Figure 20.1

The new universe of EMU Eurozone pan-European stock indices: Dow Jones (DJ) Euro STOXX indices and the relations between them. DJ Euro STOXX 50 is a top-50-blue-chip index in the EMU Eurozone, whereas DJ STOXX 50 is a selection of top-50 blue chips all across Europe, including the 10 EMU Eurozone countries (Austria, Belgium, Finland, France, Germany, Ireland, Italy, the Netherlands, Portugal, and Spain). Stock ranking is based on market cap and turn-over. The broad EMU Eurozone market index DJ Euro STOXX has 330 stocks, whereas the broad pan-European DJ STOXX index has 660 stocks. These indices are building blocks for interesting pan-European and pan-EMU Eurozone macro trades. Sector indices are also available for the new EMU Eurozone.

Table 20.1   Comparative Analysis Euro STOXX 50 vs. STOXX 50

DJ STOXX Indices			
Country weighting	Euro STOXX 50	STOXX 50	Euro STOXX 50–STOXX 50
Austria			0.00%
Belgium	2.26%		2.26%
Denmark			0.00%
Finland	1.65%	1.14%	0.51%
France	22.98%	11.61%	11.37%
Germany	26.67%	17.64%	9.03%
Greece			0.00%
Ireland	0.71%		0.71%
Italy	11.16%	6.28%	4.88%
Netherlands	25.96%	16.84%	9.13%
Norway			0.00%
Portugal	0.69%		0.69%
Spain	7.92%	4.77%	3.16%
Sweden		3.40%	−3.40%
Switzerland		14.26%	−14.26%
United Kingdom		24.07%	−24.07%

Sector weighting	Euro STOXX 50	STOXX 50	Euro STOXX 50–STOXX 50
Auto	4.66%	2.42%	2.24%
Bank	10.33%	10.80%	−0.47%
Basic resources			0.00%
Chemical	4.04%	1.52%	2.52%
Conglomerates	2.28%	2.53%	−0.26%
Construction	0.94%		0.94%
Consumer cyclical	0.54%		0.54%
Consumer noncyclical	3.27%	3.56%	−0.29%
Energy	16.12%	13.86%	2.26%
Financial services	4.77%	5.17%	−0.40%
Food and beverage	4.43%	7.68%	−3.25%
Industrial	2.81%	1.46%	1.35%
Insurance	12.71%	11.96%	0.75%
Media	0.73%	0.68%	0.05%
Pharmaceutical	1.16%	11.76%	−10.60%
Retail	2.24%	2.34%	−0.10%
Technology	7.67%	7.45%	0.23%
Telecom	15.82%	13.65%	2.17%
Utility	5.46%	3.15%	2.31%

Note: Comparative analysis performed by the author using April 1998 data provided by Deutsche Bourse.

United Kingdom and Switzerland. There is already a macro spread that is tradable given the recent pan-European launch of Euro STOXX 50 and STOXX 50 futures:

Dow Jones Euro STOXX 50 futures/Dow Jones STOXX 50 futures

In view of our previous country- and sector-weight analysis, this macro spread is closely related to the long/short basket of stock index futures:

Long CAC 40 (France), DAX (Germany),
EOE (Netherlands) futures/

Short FTSE 100 (UK), SMI (Switzerland) futures

This is very clearly shown in Figure 20.3, whereas Figure 20.2 shows how, based on our comparative sector analysis, the same spread previously considered between the top-50 EMU blue chips index future and the top-50 pan-European (including EMU) blue chips index future is shown to track very closely the pan-European sector spread

Long European car manufacturing stocks/Short European
pharmaceutical stocks

This is because all car manufacturers are in the EMU (France: Renault, Peugeot; Germany: Volkswagen, Daimler, BMW; Italy: Fiat) and the biggest European pharmaceutical giants are outside the EMU (United Kingdom: Glaxo-Wellcome, SmithKline Beecham; Switzerland: Roche, Novartis). The EMU/Europe top-50 blue chips futures spread discussed earlier is important because it gives an idea of the relation between the top of the Euromarket stock markets and the corresponding top of the non-EMU stock markets, thus defining clearly the relation between the internal universe and the external environment of the Eurozone stock markets. We still use the plural *markets*, but very soon pan-European integration will lead to several EMU stock markets where all the main EMU stocks will trade simultaneously in the same currency, the Euro.

One of the most fascinating observations on EMU/non-EMU stock market relations is that EMU stock markets are like the tip of an "iceberg" in a non-EMU (outside EMU) "ocean," so any reaction emerging in the big "ocean" takes a while to diffuse to produce the same mirror-image focused reaction on the tip of the "iceberg" (for example, if the "ocean" heats up, after a while the tip of the "iceberg" starts melting down). In fact, the white rectangle in Figure 20.1 is like a cube of ice, and the big gray rectangle is the water or ocean it floats in. What we are missing from this metaphor is not necessarily the *Titanic* but a sort of macroeconomic information "ship" that can travel across the ocean to the iceberg and back (perhaps the "waves of the ocean" can be thought of as a vehicle transporting the macro information). Figure 20.4 is only a tiny, slightly elaborated and studied situation in which the blue chips/mid-caps ratio in the whole of Europe, or a related ratio

(1) Dow Jones Euro STOXX 50/Dow Jones Euro STOXX

acts as a leading indicator for the blue chips/mid-caps ratio in Euromarket, or for the related ratio

(2) Dow Jones STOXX 50/Dow Jones STOXX.

Mid-caps here means, of course, stocks of companies with medium market capitalization. We can see in 1993 and 1996 how ratio 2 leads the way for ratio 1 up in 1993 and then down in 1996. Ratio 2 has already recovered in 1998 and, if we are right, at some later stage ratio 1 should follow it up. This gives a good indicator for a possible macro trade.

We presented in Chapter 19 an example of EMU macroeconomic mispricing that involved ratio 1 just defined and the ratio ECU/US $ as a temporary substitute for Euro/US $, a pan-European exchange rate with respect to the US dollar. Traditionally ratio 1 speaks of the strength of internationally diversified Euro companies (exporters), often major

Figure 20.2

European auto stocks/European pharmaceuticals tracks the spread between DJ Euro STOXX 50 and DJ STOXX 50 stock indices (futures are available to implement this ratio). The new EMU market will be underweight in pharmaceuticals (which are mainly in the United Kingdom and Switzerland) and definitely overweight in auto stocks (Renault, Peugeot, Daimler, BMW, Volkswagen are all in EMU).

(Original strategy and figure designed and presented by the author using Datastream database and graphics.)

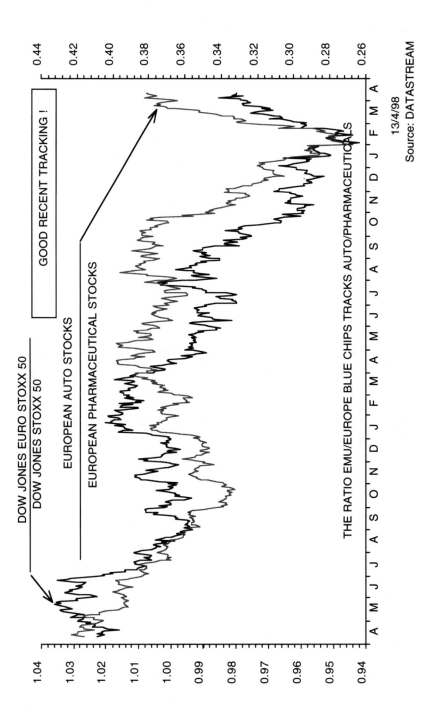

DOW JONES EURO STOXX 50

DOW JONES STOXX 50

EUROPEAN AUTO STOCKS

EUROPEAN PHARMACEUTICAL STOCKS

GOOD RECENT TRACKING !

THE RATIO EMU/EUROPE BLUE CHIPS TRACKS AUTO/PHARMACEUTICALS

13/4/98
Source: DATASTREAM

Figure 20.3

EMU vs. Europe (DJ Euro STOXX 50/DJ STOXX 50) and the stock indices basket spread (France-CAC 40, Germany-DAX, Netherlands-EOE) vs. (UK-FTSE, Switzerland-SMI).

(Original strategy and figure designed and presented by the author using Datastream database and graphics.)

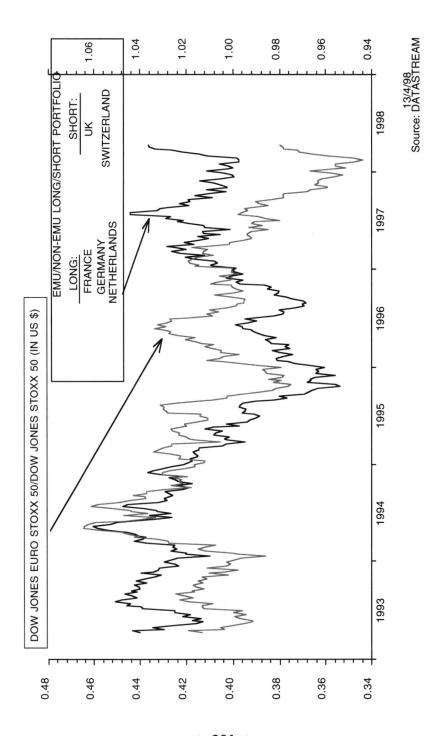

DOW JONES EURO STOXX 50/DOW JONES STOXX 50 (IN US $)

EMU/NON-EMU LONG/SHORT PORTFOLIO

LONG:
FRANCE
GERMANY
NETHERLANDS

SHORT:
UK
SWITZERLAND

13/4/98
Source: DATASTREAM

Figure 20.4

Blue chips/mid-caps in all of Europe is a leading indicator for blue chips/mid-caps in the EMU Eurozone. The ratio DJ STOXX 50/DJ STOXX gives an indication of the relative strength of European blue chips versus European mid-cap stocks. The equivalent of this spread in the EMU Eurozone is DJ Euro STOXX 50/DJ Euro STOXX. The figure shows how any change in the balance between blue chips and mid-caps in Europe as a whole acts as a signal and a leading indicator for the same change to happen within the EMU Eurozone universe. Watching relations between assets in Europe as a whole (including the EMU), one gets advance signals, predictions, and expectations for the same delayed relations in EMU.

(Original strategy and figure designed and presented by the author using Datastream database and graphics.)

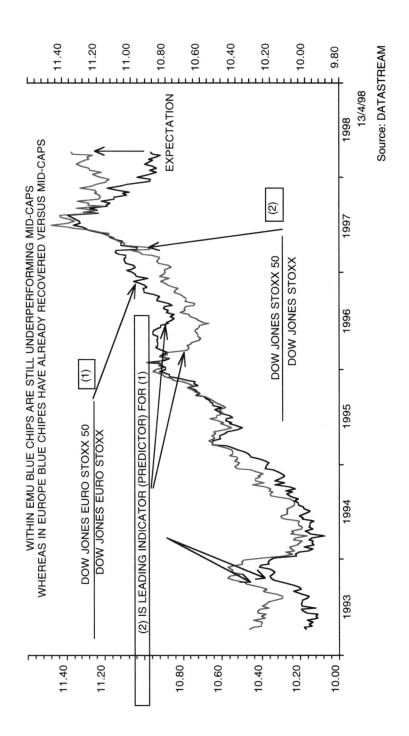

WITHIN EMU BLUE CHIPS ARE STILL UNDERPERFORMING MID-CAPS
WHEREAS IN EUROPE BLUE CHIPES HAVE ALREADY RECOVERED VERSUS MID-CAPS

DOW JONES EURO STOXX 50
DOW JONES EURO STOXX

(1)

(2) IS LEADING INDICATOR (PREDICTOR) FOR (1)

DOW JONES STOXX 50
DOW JONES STOXX

(2)

EXPECTATION

Source: DATASTREAM

13/4/98

blue chips. This strength is in large part dependent on US dollar strength, with the exception of 1998 when this interpretation was widened to accommodate for the suffering Asian exports and the result was the gap in Figure 19.2. Major macroeconomic mispricings can be detected and studied within the EMU by using the general framework of Dow Jones STOXX indices and our macroeconomic arbitrage method presented so far.

Chapter 21

Macro Arbitrage of Industrial Production Mispricings in Equity Markets

Macro Arbitrage: Industrial Production

This chapter continues the unveiling of deeper and fuller uses of the classic macroeconomic indicators beyond the traditional interpretations in terms of the state of growth and inflation leading to interest rates and currency conclusions.

The industrial production index is an indicator of the output of manufacturing, utility, and mining companies. Its importance in directional macro trading is now universally accepted, but as we will point out next it is only the "tip of the iceberg" in terms of how much more can be extracted out of its structural composition. The stereotypical use of this macro indicator is as a detector of inflation via excessive growth. Typical market reaction used to be bullish on bonds and stocks if industrial production was lower than expected in a market dominated by inflationary fears and excessive growth or overheating. The Asian crisis reversed this: suddenly the fears that the U.S. Federal Reserve Bank will raise interest rates disappeared and were replaced by fears that growth will slow down and so will corporate earnings. So if the industrial production index is lower than expected, sell equities because Asia is causing slowing growth. However this is still seen as noninflationary by bonds, which go up on such data. That is how the traditional positive correlation between bonds and equities collapsed in unusual negative territory on lower-than-expected industrial production during the recent Asian crisis (see also Figure 4.3). That is where traditional directional macro trading stops when it comes to making use of industrial production.

Macro Arbitrage: Industrial Production

What about the web of relations between its components (for example, between the industrial production of autos and the industrial production of auto parts) and the corresponding sectors of the stock market (autos and auto parts)? Despite its notoriously volatile nature, U.S. industrial production of autos, after perhaps some smoothing (using moving averages) and even filtering, gives an accurate indication of the strength of this sector. It is, of course, a quantitative indicator rather than a qualitative one, so one needs to ensure that the comparative dynamics of margins in the auto and auto parts industries are comparable before expecting to have the same relation that exists between industrial production of autos and industrial production of auto parts being reflected in the relation between the two corresponding sectors of the stock market. Figure 21.1 is a general raw attempt to macro arbitrage mispricings of the ratio between U.S. industrial productions in related industries and the corresponding ratio of U.S. stock market sectors (sectors of S&P 500). In the United States, industrial production is very volatile as can be seen from the spikes at the beginning of 1990 and 1996, which should be filtered and carefully checked. However one can see enough tracking between the macro ratio and the market price ratio. The last quarter of 1994 and the beginning of 1995 saw the wide opening of a macroeconomic mispricing gap, giving a macroeconomic arbitrage opportunity for a three-month trade: long auto stocks/short auto parts stocks. One should double check the conclusions emanating from the analysis of Figure 21.1 by an analysis of a sort of macroeconomic global measure of industry margins (one potential candidate for this margins measure when there is data available is the difference consumer price index minus producer price index [CPI – PPI]), which can in some cases bring the qualitative component to be combined with industrial production as the quantitative component to yield a full quantitative/qualitative measure suitable for macroeconomic ratios and related comparisons.

Figure 21.1

Macroeconomic arbitrage investment strategy based on industrial production mispricing in the spread (ratio) U.S. auto stocks/US auto parts and equipment manufacturer stocks. The ratio between the industrial production of autos and the industrial production of auto parts and equipment influences the sector ratio auto stocks/auto parts and equipment stocks. A clear divergence appeared at the end of 1994 and corrected after one year. This was a macro investment opportunity overweight autos/underweight auto parts from the second quarter to the last quarter of 1995.

The following indices were used:

S&P 500 car manufacturers sector index	*S&P auto parts sector index*
Chrysler	Cooper Tire
Ford Motor	Dana Corp
General Motors	Echlin
	Goodyear
	ITT
	and others

(Original strategy and figure designed and presented by the author using Datastream database and graphics.)

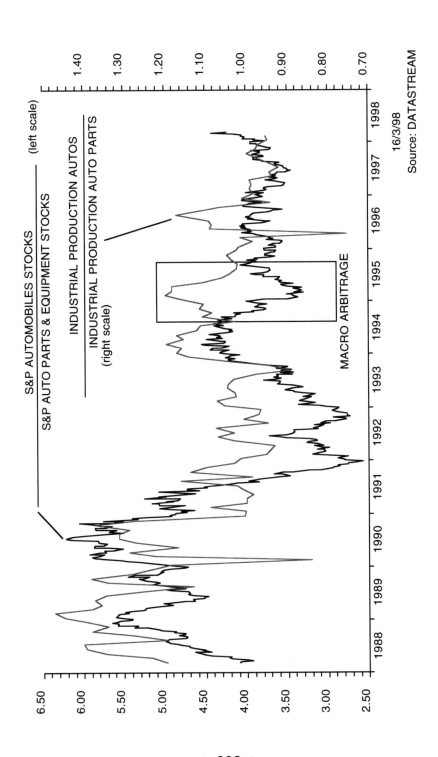

Source: DATASTREAM

16/3/98

S&P AUTOMOBILES STOCKS

(left scale)

S&P AUTO PARTS & EQUIPMENT STOCKS

INDUSTRIAL PRODUCTION AUTOS

INDUSTRIAL PRODUCTION AUTO PARTS
(right scale)

MACRO ARBITRAGE

Global Financial Crisis Domino Effect Corrects Macro Mispricings

Global Crisis Corrects Macro Mispricings

T he decision to add this epilogue was made when the manuscript of this book was in an advanced editing phase, several months after being submitted to the publisher. One of the motivations to write an epilogue stems from the temptation to check the future performance of some of the macro arbitrage opportunities left open in the chapters written earlier in 1998: Have those mispricing gaps closed or have they widened even more?

The other main motivation comes from the fact that when the core of this book was written, the origins of the global financial crisis of 1998 were attributed solely to the Asian crisis (including Japan). However, during 1998 a full domino of financial and economic crises developed: the Asian crisis was followed by the Russian crisis, the Latin American crisis, and last but not least, the hedge fund crisis. One cannot imagine a more difficult, volatile, and unpredictable financial market environment to stress-test our long/short macroeconomic arbitrage strategies.

This epilogue allows the book to end on a very positive tone because the examples will prove that global financial crises have a positive side effect: dislocations produced by market turmoil due to financial and economic crises contribute to arbitraging macro mispricings by closing open gaps between markets and underlying macroeconomics. The global financial crisis domino effect can also create new such macro arbitrage opportunities, besides contributing to closing previous mispricing gaps.

Consider first the macro mispricing of the Spanish yield curve steepness (the difference between 10-year yield and short-term rates) in the spread between Spanish banks stocks and Spanish utilities. In Figure 14.2 (see page 121), a wide gap opened at the end of 1997. Despite yield curve flattening, Spanish banks continued to outperform utilities contrary to the intuitive and the historic relation shown in this figure. As is shown in Figure 14.2E (the update of Figure 14.2 with "E" for Epilogue), this gap is now closed and the mispricing has been corrected. The main catalyst for this correction was the Latin American crisis, which hit Spanish banks because they had large exposure to this geographical area. The re-allocation of equity portfolios out of banks into utilities was another factor because utilities are heavily invested in bonds and thus are more defensive, being perceived as bond sensitive and even bond proxies.

The big dollar/yen sell-off of October 1998, during the hedge fund crisis, led to the closing of the gap between the dollar/ECU exchange rate and the ratio Dow Jones Euro STOXX 50/Dow Jones Euro STOXX (relative performance of EMU top-50 blue chips). (See Figure 19.2 on page 189, and Figure 19.2E.) Another reason for this closing was that EMU blue chips recovered relative to the EMU universe, despite the weak dollar, and this was because the shift into EMU Euroland equities began in mid-1998 ahead of the 1999 EMU final stage. This equity re-allocation shift into the EMU started initially at the blue-chips level and expanded to a full-scale portfolio restructuring.

The French banks/German banks ratio (with local markets hedged out and currency adjusted) was shown in Figure 17.8 (see page 165) to have totally mispriced the effect of the Asian crisis episodes of 1997 and 1998. The Russian and Latin American crises showed again a fragile, exposed French banking sector, as opposed to the German banking sector in which resources have always been found to provide for the large exposures to Russia and Asia. The existence of these resources and the prompt transparent way to address crisis led to the substantial correction in the fall of 1998 when the mispricing gap highlighted in Figure 17.8E did close to what was anticipated in Chapter 17.

Finally, the Finnish/Swedish stock index spread analyzed in Figure 17.4 (see page 153), was not only sensitive to the Asian crisis but also

Figure 14.2E

Global financial crisis domino corrects interest rates mispricing in Spanish banks/utilities. Figure 14.2 (see page 121) showed how a wide mispricing gap opened in February 1998 between interest rates (yield curve steepness given by 10-year yield minus 3-month rate) and the Spanish banks/utilities sector price index ratio. As anticipated, this gap had to close, and it did indeed in the second half of 1998. Due to the world financial crisis (in particular in Latin America) that affected Spanish banks, investors moved away from financial stocks into more defensive stocks and bonds. Utilities are often seen as bond proxies, or at least as very sensitive to bonds, and are always perceived as more defensive and as a safe haven during stock market falls.

The following sector indices were used:

Spanish banks sector index	Spanish utilities sector index
Argentaria	Endesa
BBV	FECSA
BCH	Gas y Electricidad
Popular	Hidrocantabrico
Santander	Iberdrola
Banesto	Sevillana
Bankinter	Union Fenosa
and others	and others

(Original strategy and figure designed and presented by the author using Datastream database and graphics.)

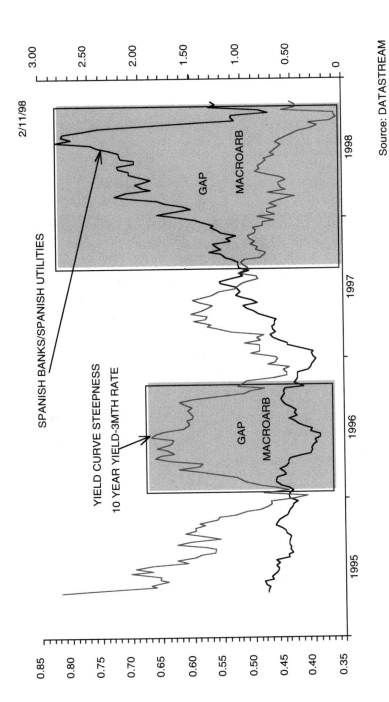

Source: DATASTREAM

Figure 19.2E

Correction of the macro mispricings of exchange rates in the EMU (Eurozone) blue chips relative performance ratio. In Figure 19.2 (see page 189), a wide mispricing of ECU/US $ (currency exchange rate) was identified in the first half of 1998 in the Dow Jones Euro STOXX 50/Dow Jones Euro STOXX ratio (Eurozone blue chips relative performance). As expected, this gap had to close, and it did indeed in October 1998 with the important contribution of a historic hedge fund, crisis-triggered, overnight sell-off in US $/Yen. Nevertheless, the pan-European relative performance of blue chips also improved gradually in the second half of 1998 making its own contribution to the closure of the mispricing gap.

(Original strategy and figure designed and presented by the author using Datastream database and graphics.)

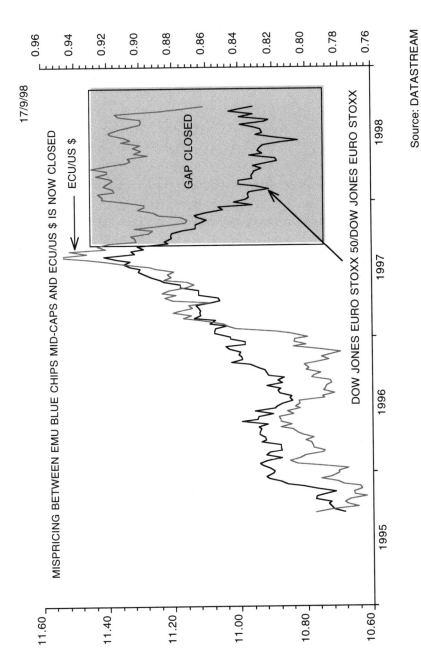

MISPRICING BETWEEN EMU BLUE CHIPS MID-CAPS AND ECU/US $ IS NOW CLOSED

17/9/98

ECU/US $

GAP CLOSED

DOW JONES EURO STOXX 50/DOW JONES EURO STOXX

Source: DATASTREAM

♦ 217 ♦

Figure 17.8E

The Russian and Latin American crises contributed to the correction of the macroeconomic mispricing of the Asian crisis in the French banks/German banks ratio (with currency adjustment and local markets hedged out [hedged with CAC 40/DAX spread]). Figure 17.8 (see page 165) showed at the beginning of 1998 the opening of a large mispricing of the Asian crisis in the French banks/German banks ratio with currency and local-markets effect hedged out. As anticipated, this mispricing had to be corrected. It took the shocks of two more financial crises (the Russian and Latin American ones) to realize and to correct this mispricing.

The following sector indices were used:

French banks sector index	German banks sector index
Bancaire	Bayerische Hypo
BNP	Bayerische Vereinsbank
CCF	Commerzbank
Credit Lyonnais	Deutsche
Natexis	Dresdner
Dexia	
Paribas	
Societe Generale	
and others	and others

(Original strategy and figure designed and presented by the author using Datastream database and graphics.)

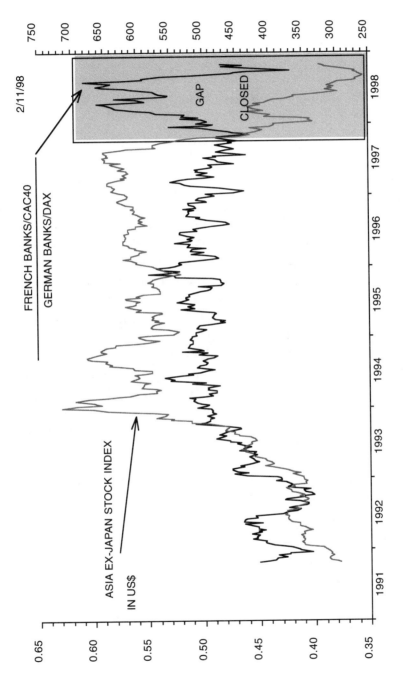

Source: DATASTREAM

♦ 219 ♦

Figure 17.4Ea

Partial mispricing of the Russian crisis in the macro ratio of equity markets Finland (FOX)/Sweden (OMX). Figure 17.4 (see page 153) showed the mispricing of the Russian crisis in the equity markets ratio Finland (FOX)/Sweden (OMX). As the global financial crisis domino progressed, the Russian financial system collapsed. This created a new mispricing in the Finnish/Swedish stock market ratio as Finland continued to outperform despite its exports and thus its economy being much more dependent on Russia. This mispricing was partially corrected in October 1998 by a sharp downward correction from the top of the highlighted channel to its bottom. However, that channel pattern created over one year was not broken because the equity reallocations into EMU Euroland from non-EMU favored Finland over Sweden (see Figure 17.4Eb).

(Original strategy and figure designed and presented by the author using Datastream database and graphics.)

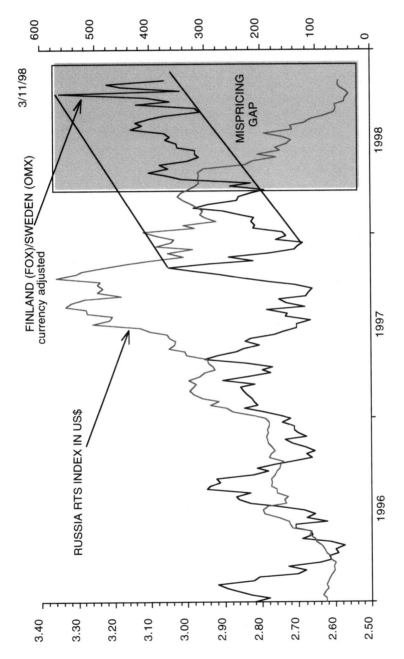

Source: DATASTREAM

Figure 17.4Eb

Asset allocation shift into EMU Euroland from non-EMU ahead of 1999 final stage of EMU compensated for Russian crisis effects on the macro ratio of equity markets Finland (FOX)/Sweden (OMX). The explanation of the persistence of a macro mispricing of the Russian crisis in the Finnish/Swedish stock market ratio is a parallel compensatory mechanism favoring Finland over Sweden. Although more exposed to Russia, Finland entered the EMU, whereas Sweden did not. The massive shift into EMU from non-EMU (shown by the outperformance of Dow Jones Euro STOXX over Dow Jones STOXX) led to the Finnish stock market outperformance over the Swedish one, despite Finnish exports being much more dependent on Russia.

(Original strategy and figure designed and presented by the author using Datastream database and graphics.)

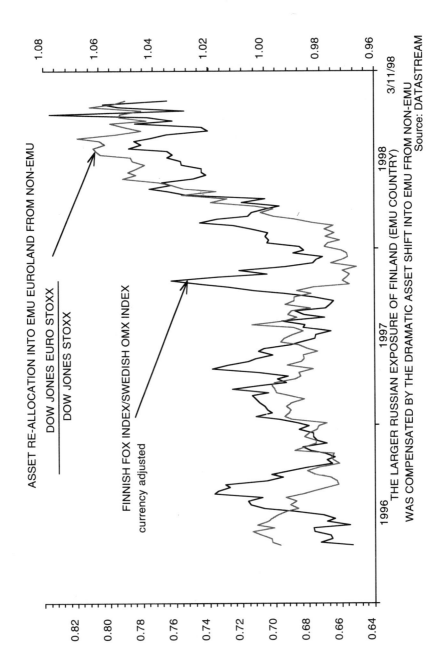

ASSET RE-ALLOCATION INTO EMU EUROLAND FROM NON-EMU

DOW JONES EURO STOXX
―――――――――――
DOW JONES STOXX

FINNISH FOX INDEX/SWEDISH OMX INDEX
currency adjusted

THE LARGER RUSSIAN EXPOSURE OF FINLAND (EMU COUNTRY)
WAS COMPENSATED BY THE DRAMATIC ASSET SHIFT INTO EMU FROM NON-EMU
Source: DATASTREAM

to the Russian crisis: the contribution to the Finnish gross domestic product (GDP) of Finnish exports to Russia is bigger than the contribution to the Swedish GDP of Swedish exports to Russia. This stock index spread mispriced the Russian crisis in the same way in which it mispriced the Asian crisis exposure. However this time, this mispricing was only partially corrected (see Figure 17.4Ea). The reason for this is a compensatory effect from the equity re-allocations into EMU Euroland from non-EMU. This shift into EMU favored the Finnish stock market because Finland is in the EMU while Sweden is not. It is expected (but still surprising) to see the level of similarity between the Dow Jones Euro STOXX/Dow Jones STOXX stock index ratio and the Finnish FOX/Swedish OMX stock index ratio in Figure 17.4Eb. The rally during 1998 is a visual expression of what we called "shift into EMU from non-EMU" and explains why the negative effect of the Russian crisis was partially compensated for by this positive effect of the move into EMU Euroland equities.

Index

Arbitrage, 8. *See also* Macroeconomic
  arbitrage
Asian crisis, 139–168
  causes of, 140–141
  contribution of Russian and Latin
    American crises to correction of
    macroeconomic mispricing of,
    218–219
  correct pricing in micro equity
    spread, 141, 144–147
  correct pricing in relative sector
    performance ratio, 143, 148–149
  correct pricing with relative value
    component, 142, 146–147
  long/short macro trading and
    investment and, 26–27, 30–33
  macroeconomic arbitrage of
    mispricing in sector price ratios,
    154, 156–157
  mispricing in French banks/German
    banks ratio, 155, 162, 164–165
  mispricing in Germany/Italy stock
    market spread, 155, 160–161
  mispricing in macro ratio of equity
    markets, 150–154
  short-term macroeconomic arbitrage
    based on, in U.S. equity market,
    154–155, 158–159
Asset allocation, shift into EMU
  Euroland from non-EMU ahead
  of 1999 final stage of EMU,

compensation for Russian crisis,
  222–223

Bonds, correlation between equities
  and, 6–27, 32–33

Consumer expenditure mispricings, in
  global market, macro arbitrage
  and, 126–131
Currency mispricings. *See* Exchange
  rates
Cyclical sector spread, 109, 112–113

Directional macro trading and investment, 14–23
  based on Euroconvergence views on
    interest rates ahead of single
    currency, 22–23
  based on macroeconomic views,
    16–17
  Euroconvergence ahead of single
    currency phase and, 18–19
  lack of correlation to macroeco-
    nomic arbitrage, 96–97, 98–99
  macroeconomic arbitrage and long/
    short macro strategies compared
    with, 51–57
  stock market rallies in Italy and
    Spain and, 20–21
Dow Jones STOXX family of stock
  indices, 193–204

Index